TEQUILA, MEZCAL & MORE

TEQUILA, MEZCAL & MORE

DISCOVER, SIP & MIX THE BEST AGAVE SPIRITS

ANNA BRUCE

With cocktails and other serving suggestions by Brooks Bailey

MITCHELL BEAZLEY

To all the agave spirits lovers and makers,
movers and shakers.

First published in Great Britain in 2025 by Mitchell Beazley,
an imprint of
Octopus Publishing Group Ltd
Carmelite House
50 Victoria Embankment
London EC4Y 0DZ
www.octopusbooks.co.uk
www.octopusbooksusa.com

An Hachette UK Company
www.hachette.co.uk

The authorized representative in the EEA
is Hachette Ireland,
8 Castlecourt Centre, Dublin 15, D15 XTP3, Ireland
(email: info@hbgi.ie)

Text and photography copyright © Anna Bruce 2025
Design and layout copyright © Octopus Publishing
Group Ltd 2025

Distributed in the US by Hachette Book Group
1290 Avenue of the Americas, 4th and 5th Floors
New York, NY 10104

Distributed in Canada by Canadian Manda Group
664 Annette St., Toronto, Ontario, Canada M6S 2C8

ISBN 978-1-78472-976-9
eISBN 978-1-78472-977-6

A CIP catalogue record for this book is available from
the British Library.

Printed and bound in China.

10 9 8 7 6 5 4 3 2 1

Commissioning Editor: Jeannie Stanley
Editor: Scarlet Furness
Copy Editor: Laura Gladwin
Art Director: Juliette Norsworthy
Designer: Geoff Fennell
Photography: Anna Bruce
Illustrator: Uriel Barragán 'Bouler'
Production Managers: Lucy Carter and Nic Jones

MIX
Paper | Supporting
responsible forestry
FSC
www.fsc.org
FSC® C008047

CONTENTS

MY JOURNEY INTO AGAVE SPIRITS

Like too many people, my earliest experience of agave spirits was cheap tequila: a yellowish liquid in a clear bottle. Fortunately, in 2008, I was lucky enough to visit a friend in Mexico, who took me to my first mezcalería (a bar specializing in mezcal). The shelves were stacked with glass jugs of this mystical-looking liquid. We were poured large servings, meant for sipping – definitely not shotting! Over these copitas (tasting glasses), I fell in love with the story and spirits of agave.

In July 2013 I returned to Mexico to document mezcal production. This was in response to an open callout from the Mexican Embassy in the UK, who had asked for pitches that would positively influence European perspectives of Mexico. Considering the reputation of tequila, mezcal seemed like a great way to showcase an amazing product rich with traditional skill, which spoke to topics of national pride and sustainability.

Travelling to the Oaxaca region of Mexico, my project coordinator was a little nervous about this young Brit who'd showed up for five weeks in the heartland of agave spirits. Fortunately, I was lucky to have a network in Mexico who could help me connect with brands and producers. Not only did they make me feel at home, but they also welcomed me behind the scenes of their incredible spirit production.

Since that first project, I have produced content about mezcal for numerous brands and publications. The interest and connoisseurship around agave spirits grow month by month, as do the international sales of mezcal and tequila. What was once the niche choice of passionate bartenders is now a rich category available to all.

OPPOSITE: *Brooks and me getting involved loading the agave oven with Madre Mezcal in Oaxaca.*

I met my own passionate bartender, Brooks Bailey, when he visited Mexico in 2017 to learn about agave spirits. I was photographing the same palenque, or mezcal distillery, in Ejutla, Oaxaca, for a news story. After going through the process step by step, we were treated to a barbecue lunch where the group tasted a huge range of mezcals, ranging from a casual 45% alcohol to a staggering 70%.

In a tipsy haze of agave, we went out to the fields to harvest agave at sunset. A little unsteadily, Brooks helped me level my camera as I tried to capture the low-lit scene. Romantic! A few months later I had persuaded him to leave the cocktail bar he managed, and move down to the source (of mezcal).

If you have the opportunity to visit a mezcal distillery, it can be a profound experience. Smelling cooked and fermenting agave while you try high-proof mezcal hot off the still is an experience that will stay with you – and will most likely entice you back.

Since then, we have created a life around visiting producers, designing drinks and sharing our experiences. Through our work we are fortunate to meet enthusiastic drinkers who are keen to discover the story behind the spirit. I hope that in this book we've managed to share our love of mezcal, and inspired you to discover its magic.

NOTE: In the brand directories, the cost of a bottle is indicated by dollar symbols, $ being the cheapest and $$$$ being the most expensive. Tasting notes vary from batch to batch and can be subjective, influenced by what they are paired with, the ambient environment and even your mood!

OPPOSITE, CLOCKWISE FROM TOP LEFT:
Mezcal tasting at Rambhá.

Grapefruit and mezcal cocktail finished with aromatic burning rosemary.

Mezcal tasting at Palenque Tío Lipe in Santa Catarina Minas, Oaxaca.

Martini Splash.

SECTION I:

WHAT IS AN AGAVE SPIRIT?

IT STARTS WITH AGAVE

Before tequila and mezcal, as we know them today, were produced, there were agave spirits. These were made from different plants in different regions, cooked, fermented and distilled, usually in a small pot still. Agave, also known as maguey, has been intertwined with Mexican culture for thousands of years. Many will be surprised to know it is not a cactus, but part of the asparagus family, *Asparagaceae*. Historically seen as a gift from the gods, agave was used for medicinal purposes, for cooking and as a building material before it became the essential ingredient of an iconic spirit: mezcal.

There is no doubt that people in Mexico have been experimenting with fermenting agave for tens of thousands of years. Long before agave became known for distillates such as tequila and mezcal, the original agave drink was a fermented liquid known as pulque. This was usually made from the sap at the heart of the *Agave salmiana* (see page 34), known locally as pulquero. The sap is named aguamiel, which translates literally as 'honey water'. To make pulque, the sap is fermented, but not distilled. Distillation separates and concentrates elements in a liquid based on their boiling points. Elements such as ethanol (a desirable alcohol) are separated from the solution by heating it. Components with the lowest boiling point evaporate, leaving unwanted parts behind in the solution. The vapours are then cooled so they recondense back into a liquid.

OPPOSITE: *Blue Weber agave in Tequila, Jalisco.*

WHAT'S THE DIFFERENCE BETWEEN TEQUILA AND MEZCAL?

This is the first thing people ask me about agave spirits. A rough answer is that tequila is a type of mezcal. There was a time when mezcal was often described as the 'smoky cousin' of tequila, but in truth it is more of a forebear.

The word 'mezcal' comes from the ancient Mesoamerican language Nahuatl, which means 'cooked agave'. When the Spanish conquistadors began to distil agave drinks, they dubbed them 'vino de mezcal', with regional addendums such as 'de Tequila' (from the town of Tequila).

Although they are distilled, agave spirits have similarities to wine. Different types of agave produce different flavours in the mezcal. They can range from sweet, fruity and floral, to musty with dry minerality. Terroir (the winemakers' term for the environment in which the grapes are grown) and the skill of the master distiller significantly influence the final product.

After hundreds of years of agave spirit production throughout Mexico (much of it clandestine), the government began to create parameters for agave spirits. They created specific appellations, such as tequila, which was introduced in 1974. Almost all 100 per cent pure tequila comes from in and around the town of Tequila, and is made from one type of agave: blue Weber, or *Agave tequilana*.

It wasn't until 1994 that mezcal changed from being a local term to an official, taxable category. Mezcal is a much broader concept than tequila, has several categories within it, and can come from various states with no restrictions on agave type. Since then, other types of mezcal, such as raicilla and bacanora, have come out of the shadows, but opinions around government-sanctioned certification remain in flux.

Over generations, tequila-makers monopolized the market, industrializing their processes and making huge quantities of cheap spirit that reached global audiences. Apart from a few premium brands sold in statement bottles, mass-produced tequila was drunk, until recently, without thought in sugary cocktails, or shotted with salt, lime and a grimace.

OPPOSITE: *Tasting aged tequila (top) and blanco (unaged) mezcal (bottom).*

EXPLORING NOTIONS OF 'ANCESTRAL' AGAVE SPIRIT PRODUCTION

For tens of thousands of years, agave was eaten throughout what is now the southwestern USA and Mexico. There is archaeological evidence that it was cooked in large pits with heated stones more than 2,000 years ago. The juices of the cooked plant were then fermented. Unfortunately, there is less certainty around whether this juice was distilled.

Archaeologists have found clay pots dating from 2000–1200 BC that could have been used for distillation in Capacha burial sites in the Colima region of Mexico, and these predate the arrival of the Spanish. The Capacha ceramics, described as bean pots, bear a resemblance to double-chambered stills from China. These Chinese stills are definitively known to have produced distilled alcoholic beverages in the 12th century.

In 2009, Mexican ethnobotanist Daniel Zizumbo-Villarreal conducted an experiment to see if it was technically possible to use these pots to distil alcohol. A local expert in traditional methods of cooking beans was

brought in to demonstrate how long it would take to cook beans in the pots. Using that as a time guide, he distilled a fermented agave mash for two hours in the pot. It was a success, although the quantity was minimal.

However, there is still a lack of chemical-residual evidence that agave distillation took place. In 2019, Dr Patrick McGovern used advanced biomolecular archaeology techniques to try to find organic compounds in the Capacha vessels, particularly looking for signs of agave or alcohol. The resulting experiments gave no evidence for agave being present inside the vessels, let alone as a distillate.

One established viewpoint is that clay pot distillation arrived in Mexico with Filipino people during the Spanish colonial period. Between 1565 and 1815, Filipinos and Mexicans sailed between Mexico and the Philippines as sailors, soldiers, enslaved people and prisoners, assisting Spain in trade between Asia and the Americas. Ancestral-style mezcal production (see pages 43 and 88) is sometimes called Filipino style.

Either way, clay pot distillation has existed in Mexico since at least the 16th century. Even if predated Europeans in Mexico, further innovations were likely transferred to locals from newly arrived distillers.

OPPOSITE: *Clay pot stills for ancestral-style mezcal production.*

BELOW: *Preparing the traditional pit oven for an agave cook in San Pablo Huixtepec, Oaxaca, where they produce Lost Explorer mezcal.*

THE LOVERS' LEGEND

Agave is often described as the plant of a thousand uses, as it offers food, drink, clothing and shelter. Some even go as far as to say that this plant was a gift from the gods. It is appropriate that this generous plant is associated with Mayahuel, Aztec goddess of agave, and one of several goddesses of fertility.

The name Mayahuel comes from the Nahuatl words metl, which means 'maguey' (an alternative word for agave) and yohualli, 'round', so together it translates to 'one who surrounds the maguey'. As well as being a symbol of sustenance, Mayahuel is associated with the artistic temperament, perhaps inspired by the influence of agave spirits.

In the ancient codices from Mesomamerica, Mayahuel is depicted giving birth, symbolizing her fertility. She holds a vase that contains pulque, the ferment of life. On the walls of Oaxaca City, and in mezcal bars around the world, it is common to see murals of Mayahuel. She usually appears seated, with what could be a throne of agave around her.

The most famous story about agave begins with a great love that grew between Mayahuel and Quetzalcoatl, the plumed serpent, who is considered to be the creator of the world and humanity. Mayahuel was the ward of Tzitzimitl, a cunning goddess of the sky who devoured light. One day, Quetzalcoatl ascended to the heavens in order to fight the goddess. He did not find her, but instead found Mayahuel, whom he rescued.

Quetzalcoatl and Mayahuel fell in love, but Tzitzimitl was furious. The couple was forced to run from her. Eventually there was nowhere else to hide, so Quetzalcoatl turned the lovers into trees. For a time, these two trees stood beside one another, and when the wind blew they were caressed by each other's leaves.

Sadly, there was no hiding from the reach of the sky goddess Tzitzimitl. She struck one of the trees with a bolt of lightning, shattering it into thousands of shards and killing Mayahuel. Overcome with grief, Quetzalcoatl took the splinters that were Mayahuel and scattered them across Mexico, shedding tears over her remains. Where pieces of Mayahuel fell to earth, the first agave grew. Quetzalcoatl went on to avenge his lover by killing Tzitzimitl, returning light to the world.

Stories help to make sense of ideas we struggle to explain. The way humanity came to consume agave is one of those questions, as the plant cannot

OPPOSITE: *Rosario Ángeles of Rambhá mezcal in front of the iconic mural in her palenque.*

be eaten raw, but must be cooked. The tree that was Mayahuel could represent the tall agave flower. Perhaps the lightning bolt did hit the 'tree', cooking the heart below and releasing its sweet sugars.

TLACUACHE GIVES MEZCAL TO HUMANITY

Quetzalcoatl, god of the wind and lover of Mayahuel, is imagined as a feathered serpent. His name is a combination of the Nahuatl words quetzal (the emerald plumed bird) and coatl (serpent). He is said to have discovered corn with the help of a giant red ant that led him to a mountain packed full of grain and seeds. He is also associated with the tlacuache (tlah·kwah·cheh), or opossum.

Perhaps surprisingly, the opossum is intertwined in the story of agave spirits. Unlike rabbits, eagles or jaguars, the opossum doesn't have a powerful status. Rather, it is shunned by people and animals alike. However, this characteristic goes on to be its saving grace. Just as Prometheus in Greek mythology stole fire from the gods, the opossum is the animal that brought fire to humans, along with agave spirits. It is considered a thief, but in a beneficial way, like the story of English cultural hero Robin Hood.

In this telling of the story, shared with me by Read Spear from Cuentacuentos Mezcal, the gods are underworld deities who are always celebrating, while the humans look on with envy and desire. The humans ask their animal friends for a way to steal these things from the deities, but none of them is up to the task. Not the jaguar, not the rabbit, nor the eagle. Eventually, the opossum speaks up, saying, 'You did not ask me. That is because everyone underestimates me. If they think of me at all, they think that I am ugly, incompetent and small. But I can fool the deities.'

Having volunteered, the opossum goes up to the deities' fire circle, observing them as they enjoy their mezcal. One of the deities says, 'Let's have some fun with this guy,' and invites the opossum to join them. 'Hey, viejito [little old man], come here, sit by the fire and drink with us!' So the opossum goes to dance and drink with the deities around their fire. The deities ply him with mezcal to get him drunk, but instead of drinking it, he hides it in his pouch.

After some time spent sneaking mezcal into his pouch, the opossum pretends to be inebriated. This amuses the deities, so they serve him more. Playing the part of a drunken fool to the crowd, the opossum pretends to be so drunk that he can no longer walk, and stumbles towards the fire. He lets his tail fall into the fire, igniting it. This, of course, causes the deities to fall over laughing. They yell at him: 'Time to go home, viejito! You have had enough, now go!' With his pouch full of mezcal and his tail on fire, the opossum runs back to the humans, and ever since, people have been able to enjoy mezcal, fire and fiesta. Their nights are filled with warmth, light and the joy of good drink, and they share their stories with one another.

Spear explained that the legend of the opossum evolved during times of hardship in Mexico. He believes that the deities represent Spanish colonialism, while the opossum represents the characteristics of the Mexican people: smart, resourceful, and (critically) underestimated. Thanks to this creature's efforts, the people are relieved from privation and can enjoy life. So raise a glass to the tlacuache – a cunning opossum!

LEFT AND ABOVE: *Illustrations of the tlachuache legend designed by César Canseco for Cuentacuentos, which feature on the brand's bottles.*

DENOMINATION OF ORIGIN

For hundreds of years, the term 'mezcal', or 'vino de mezcal' was almost synonymous with agave distillate. As with wine, though, it was eventually allocated a specific denomination of origin – mezcal de Tequila, for example.

A denomination of origin, often shortened to DO (and sometimes referred to as an appellation of origin), is a special kind of classification for an edible product. It protects geographical status, referring to products from a particular region or town that show qualities or characteristics of that area, including both the natural and human factors. DOs have no legal authority outside the country in which they are issued, although foreign countries that enter into trade agreements usually include protections for items with established DOs.

The first DO ever awarded is thought to have been to Chianti, developed by the Medici family in 18th-century Italy. The most famous DOs include Scotch whisky, Cognac, Champagne, Camembert and Ibérico ham. Currently, Mexico has allocated DOs for four agave spirits: tequila, mezcal, raicilla and bacanora. Sotol also has a DO, which, although not an agave spirit as it is made from a different plant family, is made in a similar way.

The Official Mexican Standards known as NOMs (Normas Oficiales Mexicanos) regulate all goods and services in Mexico. Specific NOMs for tequila and mezcal are NOM 006 and NOM 070 respectively, which define what can or can't be involved in the making of these agave spirits.

These NOMs are carried out as certification by a private regulatory board. Once certified, each bottle will receive a four digit number that denotes the specific distillery.

In the tequila industry they refer to 'the powerhouse', known more properly as the Consejo Regulador del Tequila (CRT). Mezcal is more complicated, with several boards federally recognized to offer certification. With over 1,400 registered brands but only around 140 approved distilleries in Mexico, the NOM serves as a valuable tool for figuring out which agave spirit comes from which producer.

Mexico's first DO was for mezcal de Tequila. Officially awarded in 1974, the DO recognized a variety of mezcal made in the town of Tequila, in the Jalisco region, which became known simply as tequila. It has to be made in defined regions, using blue Weber agave, and bottled in Mexico.

ABOVE: *Rows of blue Weber agave growing in the region of Tequila, Jalisco.*

Federal regulations control many aspects of tequila production, including which agave plants can be used, where it's made and bottled, and even what's included on the label.

In 1994, a DO was defined for the overall concept of mezcal. Unlike tequila, 'mezcal' does not denote a place, but is a term that comes from the Nahuatl for cooked agave. As previously mentioned, originally almost all agave spirits throughout Mexico were mezcals. However, to begin with the DO extended only to the states of Oaxaca, Guerrero, San Luis Potosí, Zacatecas and Durango.

Over the years, other states have been added, including Tamaulipas, Guanajuato, Puebla, Michoacán and Sinaloa. Within these states, geography, production method and agave species vary greatly, raising some concerns about whether it is appropriate to allocate a DO at all (see Sara Bowen's book *Divided Spirits* for a more in-depth treatment).

DENOMINATIONS OF ORIGIN FOR AGAVE SPIRITS

MEZCAL

1 Oaxaca
2 Puebla
3 Guerrero
4 Michoacán
5 Guanajuato
6 San Luis Potosí
7 Zacatecas
8 Durango
9 Tamaulipas
10 Sinaloa

TEQUILA

1 Jalisco
2 Nayarit
3 Tamaulipas
4 Guanajuato
5 Michoacán

SOTOL

1 Chihuahua
2 Coahuila
3 Durango

BACANORA

1 Sonora

RAICILLA

1 Jalisco
2 Nayarit

Mezcal's DO has led to great positives for the spirit, including a consumer shift away from 'big brand' tequila to an interest in small-batch, family-produced mezcals, while agave spirits in general are better understood worldwide, led by the term 'mezcal'.

However, many see major pitfalls in the certification of selected producers within the regulations of what can be called mezcal. These connoisseurs see the DO and regulations benefiting big producers who can afford the long and costly process, while exploiting the authentic small-batch mezcaleros (mezcal makers) for the identity of mezcal.

Within the NOM 070, there are three subdivisions. In ascending price order, these are mezcal, artisanal mezcal and finally ancestral mezcal.

'Mezcal' is the loosest definition and allows the use of some industrial methods. 'Artisanal mezcal' covers the broadest set of producers, encompassing most mezcal brands on the market, who follow a generally understood traditional style of mezcal production.

'Ancestral mezcal' refers to intensely traditional mezcal made in clay pot stills. Only a handful of distilleries across Mexico – primarily in Oaxaca – claim this label. Unfortunately, the 'ancestral' definition excludes many mezcaleros that could be considered ancestral, especially in states outside Oaxaca.

Some iconic brands, such as Real Minero (see page 123), are choosing to remove the word 'mezcal' from their labels. This is not to say they are unregulated: they still require lab tests to assess quality. It is a reaction to the cost, complexity and political engagement entailed by certification. They present themselves instead as destilado de agave (distilled from agave). Emerging brands such as Sin Gusano, which is focused on limited-edition batches from a range of producers, also do not certify as mezcal.

In the market for even more niche agave spirits, there are also brands, such as La Venenosa (credited with raising the profile of raicilla, see page 151), who have chosen to stay outside the rules and regulations defined by the boards of certification. At the other end of the spectrum, there are even some tequila producers, such as the brand Caballito Cerrero (see page 145), that are questioning whether to certify at all.

Fortunately, the names raicilla, mezcal and tequila convey more than certification. These names mean tradition, family, pride and spirit.

AGAVE AND THE ENVIRONMENT

WHAT IS AN AGAVE?

The key to a delicious agave spirit is – of course – the agave. 'Without maguey there is no mezcal' is a phrase often heard among the mezcal-sipping community. The last decade has seen this community grow rapidly, drawing in consumers who are keen to understand the raw material behind their favourite drink.

The word 'agave' comes from the ancient Greek agaué, meaning 'admirable, illustrious or brilliant'. The agave plant is part of the *Asparagaceae* family, and therefore a distant cousin of asparagus, which becomes evident when you see agave plants' tree-like flowers, called quiotes. Agave will only produce a flower once in its life, at the point of maturation. After this, the plant will start to die, whether it is harvested or not.

Agaves are famously tough. Over millions of years, they have evolved to survive harsh desert conditions, and they fiercely protect the water they are able to obtain. Today there are hundreds of species of agave, around 40 of which are regularly used to make spirits. Each has its own unique flavour profile, influenced by the specific terroir.

Soil is where terroir begins. Mineral-rich soils influence the development of ingredients used in spirit production, and shape the aroma and taste of the spirits. The trace elements absorbed by agaves contribute to their unique characteristics, giving each spirit a sense of place.

OPPOSITE: *Flowering tepeztate at Rancho Cebú in Tlacolula de Matamoros, Oaxaca.*

Agaves' favourite habitat is the volcanic soil of Mexico, where this plant has been treasured for generations. Agaves can be found throughout Mexico's mountains and valleys, from northern deserts to southern coasts. It took me a few scrapes to get familiar with this beautiful but challenging plant. My first trip to see a harvest was at dawn, and I was so caught up in the moment that, leaning in to get a clearer picture, I impaled my thigh on the spiny tip of the sword-like agave leaves. Only when I was offered mezcal to clean the wound did I notice the streaks of blood running down my leg.

These succulent plants are not to be confused with cacti, or aloe vera, similar though they appear. The viscous sap of aloe vera can cure a rash, whereas agave sap will cause one, as I found out after making the poor decision to wear shorts to climb a heap of fresh-cut agave hearts. My legs felt like they were on fire. Yet again mezcal came to the rescue, as the mezcalero poured it all over the rash. This was one of many experiences that give credit to the famous saying 'Para todo mal, mezcal – para todo bien también' (For everything bad, mezcal – for everything good, also mezcal).

TYPES OF AGAVE

Agave comes in many shapes and sizes, all characterized by a formation of thick, fibrous leaves tipped with spines. There are over 200 species worldwide, 75 per cent of which are found in Mexico, with a quarter of those found in Oaxaca state, most of which are used in spirit production.

Species of agave range from the pretty little rosettes of tobalá, to the palm-like *Agave karwinskii* and monumental arroqueño, which can grow to over 3 metres (10 feet) before it matures. Whether espadín in cultivated rows, *A. cupreata* wild in the forests of Michoacán or tepeztate hanging off cliffs in the hills of Oaxaca, these majestic plants have mastered their environment.

How, where and which agave is grown has a huge impact on the final spirit. Each species takes a different amount of time to mature, or flower. The quickest to mature are the cultivated species, from which almost all exported agave spirits are made. With intensive farming, *A. angustifolia* varieties (such as espadín and tequilana) can be ready to flower in around five years. Left to their own devices, this could be seven to nine years.

Most common in Oaxaca, espadín accounts for somewhere between 80 and 90 per cent of mezcal production. As a domesticated plant, some people discredit espadín as less interesting than its 'wild' counterparts. However, this agave is great at expressing the terroir in which it is grown. Since it is simple in flavour, espadín is also a good agave to try first in a range.

Tequilana, better known as blue Weber, is similar to espadín in most essential ways – size, growth time and yield – except, as the common name suggests, the skin is blue-tinged, compared to espadín's silvery hue.

Other varieties such as tobalá and arroqueño, and species such as *A. karwinskii*, are known as silvestre (wild). Typically, they take 12, 15 and 20 years respectively to mature. These timings change significantly when they are grown in domestic environments, which speed up the growing time.

Historically, agave spirit production has depended on collecting plants from the wild. This is laborious, expensive and inefficient. However, the wild varieties often produce spirits with distinctive, highly sought-after flavours.

Tepeztate is particularly slow to mature. Nicknamed 'the drunk one', its muscular, leathery leaves flail like haphazard, monstrous arms. It can take 30 years to mature, sending up vibrant yellow flowers that fill the valleys of Oaxaca in spring. These flowers are often used to decorate churches at Easter. Mezcal made from tepeztate is complex, with mineral, vegetal and fruity notes. Considering how long the plant has aged in the ground, and been exposed to environmental factors unique to where it grows, these flavours can change from batch to batch, creating fascinating vintages.

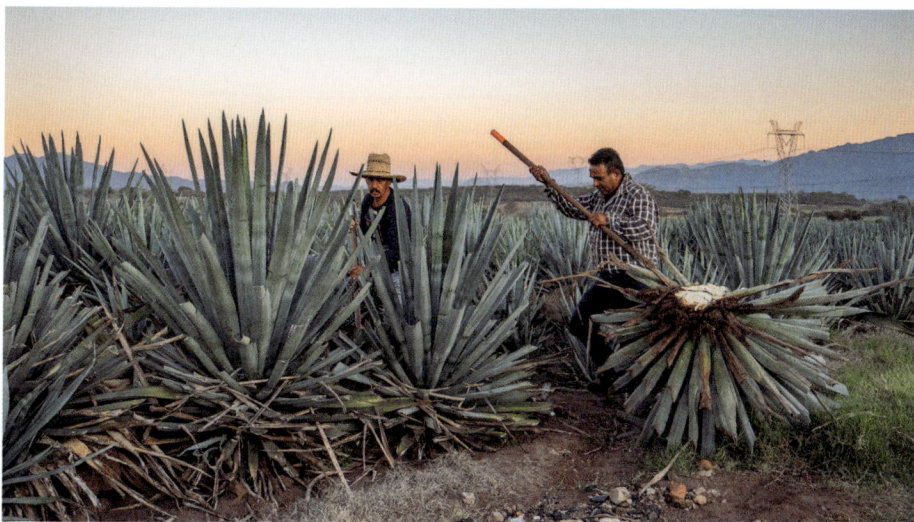

ABOVE: *Jimadors harvesting agave in Tequila.*

SPECIES OF AGAVE

Here are just a few examples of iconic agaves that are often used for distilling spirit. It is important to note that any species cultivated and cared for will mature much quicker than their wild counterparts. This will also affect the flavour, as the more stress and time it takes an agave to mature, the more closely it will guard its sugars, resulting in a much more complex flavour profile.

Each species can vary in colour, size, age and yield depending on its environment. They can also reveal different flavours depending on the region and style of the producer.

AGAVE ANGUSTIFOLIA

OPPOSITE:
Harvesting cultivated Agave angustifolia.

VARIETIES: Espadín, Blue Weber, Haw, Pacifica
AGAVE SPIRIT: Mezcal, tequila (Blue Weber), 'mixto' tequila, raicilla, bacanora

Close your eyes and think of agave. What you're imagining is probably very close to *Agave angustifolia:* very picturesque, with leaves like emblazoned swords threatening any would-be challengers that happen to pass by. Espadín in Oaxaca is a silvery green, while in Jalisco it has a heavy, dark-blue hue. The flavour profile is the simplest of all agaves: generally sweet and grassy with hints of green apple and caramelized agave notes.

Blue Weber (*A. tequilana*) naturally matures when around 7–10 years old, producing a quiote and flowers. In cultivated environments maturity could be in as little as 5 years. Like other angustifolia species, blue Weber produces numerous clones during its lifetime, genetic copies of the mother plants.

The tequila industry has been reliant on clones from this single subspecies for generations. This has left the blue Weber agave vulnerable to pests and disease. It has also led to monocrop-style growing and overharvesting.

AGAVE POTATORUM

VARIETY: Tobalá
AGAVE SPIRIT: Mezcal

Much smaller and prettier than the espadín, with more squiggly spines, these agave are known for their Fibonacci-esque rosette leaf pattern. The hearts (piñas, so called because they resemble pineapples) grow to only 40–60 kilograms (90–130 pounds), and mature in around 12 years. The plants themselves are much less dense, more 'fleshy' than other species. Mezcals made with *Agave potatorum* are usually sweet, floral and fruity.

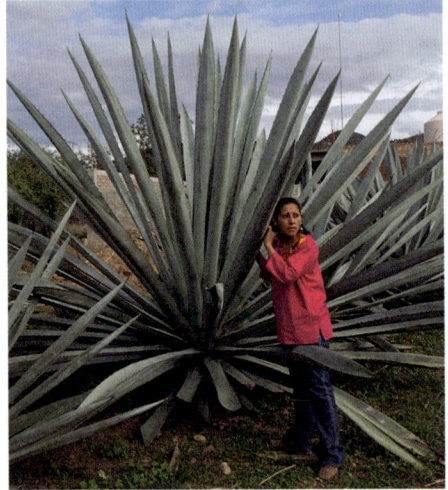

ABOVE: *Graciela Ángeles Carreño from Real Minero showing the scale of an* Agave americana.

AGAVE KARWINSKII

VARIETIES: Cirial, Cuishe/Cuixe, Bicuishe/Bicuixe, Madrecuishe, Barril, Tobaziche, Tripon, Largo
AGAVE SPIRIT: Mezcal

The species with the most names! If you find a new mezcal and do not recognize the name, it is probably an *Agave karwinskii*. Taking about 15–18 years to mature, these agaves were traditionally used as property dividers. They look more like trees with a trunk than the pineapple-ish hearts of other species. The subspecies vary in height and circumference, and some lose their leaves at the bottom, making them look even more palm-like. When shaved down for cooking, the hearts look like tall, skinny pine cones. However different the agaves are in appearance, though, the mezcals produced from them tend to have high minerality, with some even leaning towards more piney and woody notes.

AGAVE AMERICANA

VARIETIES: Arroqueño, Sierrudo, Sierra Negra
AGAVE SPIRIT: Mezcal

At first glance, *Agave americana* looks the titan ancestor of espadín, with very tall, straight, sword-like silver-green leaves. Maturing in about 15–18 years, the quiotes can reach 9 metres (30 feet). The mezcal tends to be dry, mineral and almost dusty-tasting, with a bit of a barnyard-like funk to them.

ABOVE: *A beautiful* Agave marmorata *at Universidad Autónoma Chapingo, Oaxaca.*

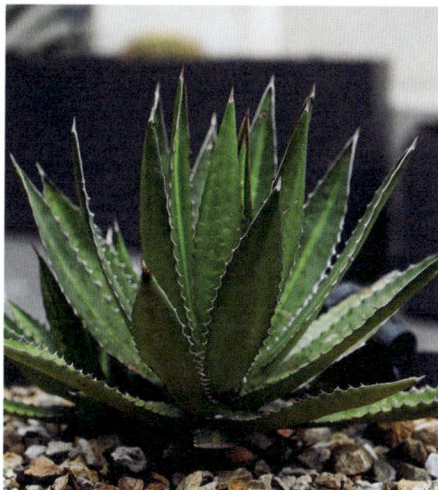

ABOVE: *Ornamental* Agave convallis *in Oaxaca.*

AGAVE MARMORATA

VARIETIES: Tepeztate/Tepextate, Becuela
AGAVE SPIRIT: Mezcal

Much less uniform than other agave species, the form of *Agave marmorata* looks both kinetic and static, almost as if flames had been frozen in time. The leaves are thick and leathery, with wide spines that look like shark teeth. It is sometimes described as el borracho (the drunk one) or the ugly duckling of agaves, as a bright yellow flower emerges from the hulking shape below. Also known for having the longest maturation time, *A. marmorata* can take 20–30 years or more to mature in the wild. The mezcal is very green with notes of fresh-cut serrano or jalapeño peppers and a briny aftertaste.

AGAVE CONVALLIS

VARIETY: Jabalí
AGAVE SPIRIT: Mezcal

The green leaves have a yellow stripe up the middle, which curves in from the edges and slightly from the end spine. This agave grows mostly in clusters, hunkered down as if in a defensive stance, which is probably responsible for its name: 'jabalí', meaning wild boar. It takes around 12 years to mature. Among mezcaleros, jabalí is known mostly for being a pain to work with. In fermentation, it is common for foam to spill over the tub, and after two distillations it can have a yellow tinge and most likely too much methanol to pass certification. Therefore, a third distillation is almost always necessary. When made correctly, however, it can be herbaceous, vegetal and creamy.

AGAVE SALMIANA

VARIETIES: Pulquero, Cimarrón, Verde
AGAVE SPIRIT: Pulque, comiteco, mezcal

This agave has wide, thick leaves that can be over 2 metres (6 feet) long, reminiscent of an *Agave americana* except for its tell-tale floppy nature. Described as the 'mother agave', Mayahuel is depicted with an *A. salmiana*, which takes 15–18 years to mature. *A. salmiana* in Oaxaca tends to produce fruity, floral mezcals, whereas in northern states they have green pepper and chilli notes.

AGAVE RHODACANTHA

VARIETIES: Mexicano, Cuishe, Mexicanito, Mexicano Verde, Dobodan, Cimarrón Amarillo
AGAVE SPIRIT: Mezcal, raicilla

A large agave with long, thin leaves that vary in colour from light green to dark grey-blue. Less uniform than espadín, its leaves appear slightly more haphazardly splayed. It matures in 7–12 years and the mezcal is reminiscent of espadín in its sweet, caramelized agave flavour, adding some fruity, spicy pepper notes.

AGAVE CUPREATA

VARIETIES: Papalote, Papalometl
AGAVE SPIRIT: Mezcal

Very similar to, and often confused with, tobalá (*Agave potatorum*), *A. cupreata* is distinguished by its copper-coloured spine and wide, light green leaves. Maturing in 7–15 years, *A. cupreata* mezcal is lightly floral with earthy stone fruit notes.

AGAVE LYOBAA

VARIETY: Coyote
AGAVE SPIRIT: Mezcal

Often confused with some types of *Agave rhodancatha*, *A. lyobaa* is believed to be a hybrid between *A. potatorum* and *A. karwinskii*. Its leaves are said to resemble the shape of the ears of a coyote, and it matures in 6–10 years. Mezcals made from *A. lyobaa* have a balance of baked fruits with spicy minerality.

ABOVE: *Harvesting wild* Agave rhodacantha *in Oaxaca.*

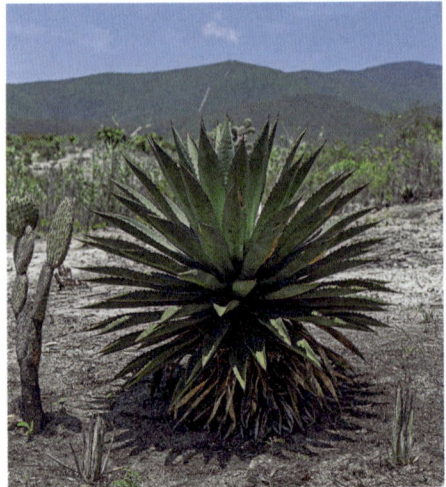

ABOVE: *An impressive* Agave lyobaa.

AGAVE MAXIMILIANA

VARIETY: Lechugilla
AGAVE SPIRIT: Mezcal, raicilla

This is one of the main agaves used to make raicilla. It looks like a close relative to *Agave potatorum*, with its rosette-style pattern and elongated, straight leaves. This variety is found in Durango, Guanajuato and Jalisco, and takes around 10 years to mature. It is small with wide green leaves that can reach up to 3 metres (10 feet) in length, and large dark spines.

AGAVE INAEQUIDENS

VARIETY: Lechuguilla
AGAVE SPIRIT: Pulque, mezcal, raicilla

This matures in around 18 years. It has large, thick green leaves with bold spikes and can reach 2.5 metres (8 feet). Lechuguilla means lettuce. It has a high yield and is also used to make pulque.

AGAVE DURANGENSIS

VARIETIES: Cenizo, Castilla
AGAVE SPIRIT: Mezcal

Appearing almost as a hybrid of tepeztate and tobalá, with ashy grey-green rosette-style leaves that sometimes undulate, *Agave durangensis* is similar to a tepeztate. It matures in around 10 years and the flavour profile is nutty, with earthy notes of fresh tobacco and leather.

AGAVE ASPERRIMA

VARIETY: Lamparillo
AGAVE SPIRIT: Mezcal

Lamparillo matures in around 15 years. It has large, light green-grey leaves that are gnarled and scoop-like, reminiscent of a tepeztate mixed with a pulquero. These are great at reproducing via rhizome, almost spilling over each other. Lamparillo mezcal is high in minerality with dry green pepper notes.

ABOVE: *Wild* Agave asperrima *catching the light in Mapimí, Durango.*

ANIMALS AND AGAVE

Animals crop up frequently in Mexican folklore. An iconic image from the world of agave spirits is the hardworking burro (donkey) with freshly harvested plants strapped to his back. Although this image indicates seriously hard work, it is also beautiful and rustic. In a time when everything is automated, fast and distant, there is something grounding in the idea of slow production connected to animals and the earth.

Many other moments throughout the production of agave spirits resonate in this way, from the bats that pollinate agave flowers to the steady work of oxen crushing cooked agave with a stone mill, the 'original rock and roll'.

Even less prominent animals play a part in the story of agave spirits: sheep and goats roam free among agave, keeping weeds in check while naturally fertilizing the agave fields. Some mezcaleros think that this livestock influences the ambient yeasts that dictate the fermentation of agave. This doesn't seem all that far-fetched if you consider the difference between a homestead-style palenque with animals moseying around, as opposed to a commercial production unit with sterile tools and walls.

Then there are the insects. During fermentation, insects of all kinds – including fruit flies and bees – swarm to the surface of the sugary mixture. The yeasts they carry change according to the time of year and the location of the distillery. They influence fermentation, which in turn affects the flavours imparted during distillation. You can tell your fermentation is finished when all the insects have left.

NEAR RIGHT: *A horse pulling the tahona to crush cooked agave at an artisanal distillery in Oaxaca.*

OPPOSITE, LEFT: *A palenque pup in Durango.*

OPPOSITE, RIGHT: *A gusano (worm).*

THE WORM

The first creature that usually comes to mind when discussing agave spirits is the worm, or gusano, that infests the living agave plant, and is sometimes steeped in a bottle of mezcal. There are many misconceptions about this worm. First of all, it's not actually a worm, but rather one of two species of moth larva that lives on the agave. This is many people's first experience of mezcal, but although it has been somewhat relegated to the status of tourist trope, there is more to it than that. Some brands, such as Mezcal Monte Alban, have leaned into it and stayed with the tradition of mezcal con gusano through thick and thin. The worm(s) add a slightly sweet, earthy flavour to the spirit, and there is also a light caramel coloration. Personally, I prefer the worm outside my mezcal, cooked and crushed up with salt and chilli.

The gusano won't make you hallucinate if you eat it. Perhaps someone got confused between the word 'mezcal' and the psychoactive mescaline which, locally, comes from the peyote cactus. That being said, mezcal aficionados often recount spiritual, if not hallucinatory, experiences when drinking mezcal. Whether or not this has to do with the worm is unclear.

MAKING AGAVE SPIRITS

HOW IS AN AGAVE SPIRIT MADE?

The complexity of flavours that can be found in agave spirits is astounding. Of course the raw material, the particular species of agave, is a leading factor, but the growing conditions are also fascinating, contributing to the unique character of each batch. The plant, though, is just the beginning.

The producer and place of production will uniquely inform the final spirit. Some compare the process to cooking, where the tiniest nuance can affect the overall flavour. However, the success of agave spirits has resulted in increased industralization and, at times, dilution of the pure agave spirit. Nonetheless, whether the production is in a small, family-run palenque or a major factory, the physicality of the process is a sight to behold.

Tonnes of agave are cut by hand, brought to the distillery and thrown into vast pit ovens, brick ovens or autoclaves. The agave change from fresh green to caramel brown as they cook, before being fermented and then finally the juice distilled. The style of each step influences the final taste.

There are beautiful, sculptural elements to the distilleries: from a machete blade leaning against a wall, clay pots and stone mills found in rustic production, to monumental copper stills found in large tequila distilleries. Staying in a palenque, among these details, is where I truly fell in love with agave spirits.

OPPOSITE: *Guillermo Martínez placing agave hearts in the oven at his family distillery in Oaxaca.*

GROWING AND HARVESTING

Agave farmers, also known as magueyeros, spend a lifetime growing agave. To do so is a commitment to the future – especially when some varieties can take a generation to mature. Traditions are passed down from one generation to the next. Over the years they learn how things work; they come to understand the plants, the earth, and how weather, pests and other creatures can impact the crop.

Whether the agave is grown from seed or clone, gathered from a field or hunted down in the wild, harvesting requires cutting the flower spike, or quiote. Typically, this happens during the dry months of the year. After the quiote is cut, the plant is left in the ground for several months, allowing it to continue drawing nutrients from the soil, which it converts to fructans (sugar), getting big and fat.

When the plant is ready, the agave farmer will slice away the leaves with a machete to reveal the heart, which sits above the ground. A sharp disc on the end of a long pole (called a coa) is then stuck between the base of the heart and the ground. A mallet is often used to hit the end of the coa, severing the roots.

Now the heart is ready to transport back to the distillery. Until recently, agave was transported from the field to palenque by donkey. Now it is commonplace to see huge trucks carrying tonnes of plants to the distilleries. For better or worse, this has hugely increased the amount of spirit that can be made.

Besides transport from the fields, mechanization does not seem to have had much impact on the harvesting of agave. The nature of the plants themselves makes mechanizing the harvest almost impossible. The human touch is necessary, from harvesting adult plants, each with a significantly different scale and weight, to extracting clones without damaging the mother plant.

OPPOSITE, FROM TOP TO BOTTOM: *The production of agave: from seedlings and clones for planting to mature plants ready to harvest*

COOKING

To make artisanal mezcal (see page 74), the hearts are brought back to the palenque and piled around the oven. Artisanal and ancestral mezcal (see page 76) are both cooked in earth or stone-lined pits known as hornos. It is fairly common for mezcaleros to have a primary oven for cooking espadín and a smaller pit for cooking wild species of agave.

A fire is built at the base of the oven and, after the fire dies down, stones are piled on the red-hot embers. These stones are themselves covered with a wet agave fibre called bagaso, which protects the raw agave and creates steam in the oven. The pit is then filled with agave hearts.

For artisanal mezcal, the cooking process tends to take between a few days and a week, depending on the ambient temperature and density of the agave. After the raw agave has been cooked, the oven

Workers at the Jicarita palenque in Santiago Matatlán, Oaxaca, breaking down agave before cooking.

An agave oven in San Dionisio Ocotepec. The mezcalero is waiting for the fire to burn off a bit before loading the oven with raw agave.

is opened to reveal caramelized agave hearts. In the ancestral process, it is standard to rest agave between cooking and crushing, to allow a mould called moho to grow. Some producers say this helps break down the fibrous agave before crushing, and it informs what is described as moho-style agave, which can have lactic, nutty or cheesy notes. This is less common with artisanal practice.

In ancestral-style productions these pits typically have a capacity of 1–5 tonnes, referring to the amount of raw agave hearts used (as opposed to 10–16 tonnes in typical artisanal palenques).

On the coast, raicilleros (makers of raicilla) may cook their agave in an earth or stone-lined underground pit, similar to those used in Oaxaca, meaning that some coastal raicillas are smokier than their mountain counterparts. For raicilla made in the mountains, above-ground adobe ovens are common. Similar to huge pizza ovens, these look like huts, with a door at the base and chimney above. They are operated by filling

the base with wood and bringing it to a roaring fire. At this point the bottom is sealed and raw agave pieces are dropped through the top opening. Once the ovens are filled with agave, they are sealed with mud.

In tequila production, masonry ovens called mampostería were introduced to replace traditional lined pit ovens. Nowadays, autoclaves, in which agaves are cooked via steam and pressure, are also common in tequila and can be found in some mezcal production. Pit-oven cooking often takes a week, whereas an autoclave can cook agave in as little as 12 hours.

Reduced cooking time can reduce processing costs, which translates into lower retail price and higher profit margin. However, increased productivity comes at a cost. The most evident is a loss of the rustic, smoky notes found in artisanal agave spirits produced using traditional roasting methods.

Most tequila distilleries today are very large, producing for many brands under one roof. To produce the volume required for multiple brands, many large tequila distilleries also employ diffusers. The diffuser is designed to remove agave sugars from the hearts without the effort of traditional cooking.

In traditional pit or brick ovens, even autoclaves, the steam generated from the hearts liquefies inulin (a prebiotic of fructans present in the roots of various plants) and breaks the chains into smaller fermentable sugar molecules. In a diffuser the inulin is liquefied by spraying the agave fibres with hot water. The water is then collected and heated in an autoclave, where the inulin is broken down into smaller sugar molecules.

Typically, whole raw hearts are loaded into the machine via conveyor belts. Once in the machine, the hearts are shredded and the pulp is washed in a solution that dissolves the agave inulin. Once the inulin is liquefied, it is separated from the pulp and pumped into large autoclaves. The diffuser is 99 per cent efficient in extracting potential fermentable sugars compared to 70 per cent when a brick oven and tahona (see page 46) are used.

OPPOSITE, TOP: *Loading a traditional pit oven at the Dulce Tentación vinata in Nombre de Dios, Durango.*

OPPOSITE, BOTTOM: *The oven at the Laguna Seca distillery in Charcas, San Luis Potosí.*

CRUSHING

In artisanal mezcal, maceration is done using a horse- or oxen-drawn stone wheel called a tahona (also known as an Egyptian or Chilean mill). Producers making ancestral mezcal (as well as raicilla) often crush by hand using wooden mallets. The cooked agave is cut into chunks using a machete, then put into wooden or stone canoes, where they are mashed into a pulp. Using a stone mill is possible but not common.

A typical practice is also to break down the cooked agave using a wood chipper, which is quicker and a lot less back-breaking than hand-crushing. This can be a little contentious within the ancestral concept, but most mezcal producers say there is no change to the final product. The mixture is now ready for fermentation.

FERMENTATION

Fermentation is nature's way of producing alcohol. It is a metabolic process in which yeast obtains energy by converting sugar into alcohol. Yeast is in the air all around us, growing on the surface of plants and fruits, and even on our own skin.

There are hundreds of yeast strains present on the leaf surface of agaves and the walls of the various distilleries throughout Mexico. There are also bacteria present throughout the process and these produce compounds such as acetic and lactic acid. The yeasts and other microbes are responsible for many of the tastes and aromas associated with agave-based drinks.

Fermentation can happen in different types of vessel, depending on the style and scale of the agave spirit production. Essentially, the vessel needs to be something that can hold liquid. For artisanal mezcal this is usually a wooden tub called a tina. Tinas are usually

OPPOSITE, CLOCKWISE FROM TOP LEFT: *Hand-crushing agave in San Juan del Río.*

A stone tahona in San Dionisio.

Guillermo Martínez loading cooked agave into the tahona at La Jicarita palenque in Santiago Matatlán, Oaxaca.

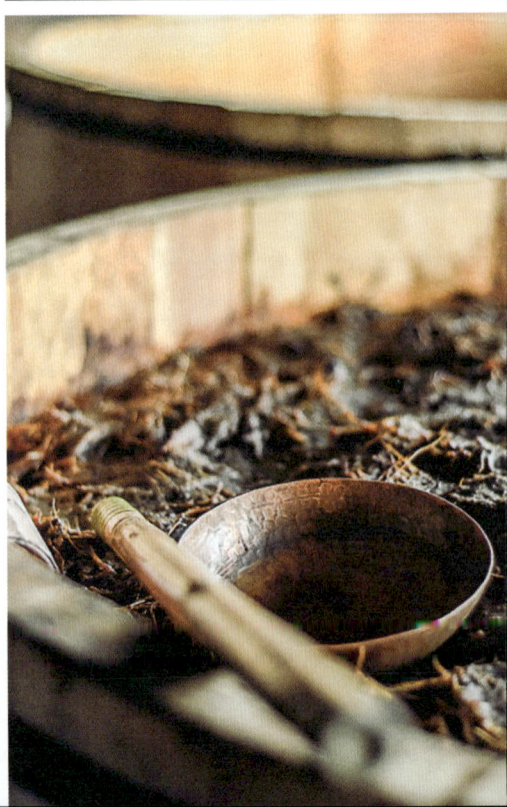

made of pine, although some of the older tubs in Oaxaca are made from sabino, a type of cypress, said to be the widest tree in the world, and found in the Oaxacan suburb of Tule. Sabinos are often found on river banks with huge gnarled buttress roots, giving rise to their nickname 'old man of the river'. Both pine and sabino have natural water-wicking properties, making them appropriate material for holding fermenting agave juice.

Tiny ancestral productions may use whatever is practical, ranging from carved-out rocks and logs, clay pots, plastic buckets or even hammock-like lengths of suspended cowhide. Bacanora mash can be fermented in the producer's vessel of choice, which can include steel oil drums, plastic tanks typically used for storing water, or underground reservoirs known as barrancos.

Most modern tequila distilleries use cultivated yeast for more control over production time and final flavour. Rather than wooden tubs, stainless steel is used, offering an easy-to-clean vessel for fermentation.

Water contains oxygen, which allows the yeasts to respire aerobically and to multiply. Once the yeasts have saturated the sugary solution, they begin to respire anaerobically. This is the process that produces alcohol as a by-product. You can see the yeast respiring as bubbles or foam form on the surface of the mash, known as the tepache. If you put your ear to the fermentation vat, you can hear the bubbles, indicating living yeast.

Tepache can be made from many plants aside from agave, and is a traditional, popular drink in its own right. If you find it in a market or on a menu, it has usually been made from fermented pineapple.

The amount of oxygen can influence the timing and final flavour of the tepache. The producer can introduce oxygen into the mix by stirring it with a long wooden pole or by adding more water, slowing down the yeast's anaerobic activity.

Once the yeast begins to work on the agave sugars, any matter in the solution rises to the top, forming a bread-like lid. This helps to insulate and protect the active ferment below. The yeast must not get too hot or cold, or it will die. However, this crust can lead to acid building up in the tepache, which would be present in the final spirit, so some producers break this up to restrict the acidity.

OPPOSITE: *Fermenting the mashed cooked agave in wooden tubs, called tinas, at Mezcal Meztlan in Santiago Matatlán, Oaxaca.*

The sweet spot for the yeast is 18–24°C (65–75°F). Hot fermentations will be finished more quickly than cooler ones. Both ends of the spectrum have funkier flavours, evident in the taste of the final spirit. These are the result of other microbes getting into the mix as the yeast dies off, making space.

This process will continue for anywhere between a day and two weeks, depending on the temperature, choice of vat, agave type and dilution.

As fermentation progresses, the tepache gets less sweet, going from a toffee-apple kind of taste to a tart vinegar flavour. When there is no trace of sweet agave flavour left, the tepache is ready to be distilled. At this point the liquid is rising in its percentage of alcohol to the level of a strong beer. Any fruit flies or other insects will also leave the top of the ferment due to the absence of sugars.

For most alcohol production, fermentation is controlled using cultivated yeast and regulated temperatures in closed vats. This helps to provide more consistency to the final batch of spirit. However, for artisanal and ancestral agave spirits the fermentation is open, so the wild yeast and ambient temperature will be different every time, creating unique flavours. Like wine, these unique batches should be celebrated as dated vintages.

Fermentation generally takes 1–3 weeks, depending on factors such as sugar content, temperature and altitude. The size and depth of the tub, as well as the ratio of water to agave can also play a role. Each agave spirit maker will also have a preferred profile for their tepache. Some prefer to leave traces of residual sugars for a sweeter, finer mezcal, whereas others prefer to have maximum fermentation, which results in a dryer, cleaner final distillate.

Bacanora has a very short distilling season in the spring, when the temperature is right for the fermentation and the rain hasn't diluted sugars in the agaves. For raicilla, fermentation generally takes 1–4 weeks. The time depends on factors such as agave sugar content, ambient temperature and altitude. If it is warm, it could take a week, but a month when it is particularly cold. As in Oaxaca, many raicilleros will stop production during the coldest months.

OPPOSITE, LEFT: *Fermentation tanks in Tequila.*

OPPOSITE, RIGHT: *The copper stills used for distilling tequila in Arandas, Jalisco.*

DISTILLATION

Once the tepache is ready, it is loaded into a still. Double-distillation is the standard in Oaxaca and most of Mexico. All mezcal should be distilled at least twice, or three times in certain situations.

COLUMN STILLS Pairs of column stills in series that can be operated continuously were a major advancement in distilling history. These stills are made up of a series of perforated plates through which increasingly pure alcohol vapours pass as impurities fall back down. The taller the column, the purer the result. The column still is highly efficient and can produce cleaner spirits than other stills. While there are some tequilas that still use alembic-style and copper pot stills (see page 53), many tequila producers distil using column stills.

OIL DRUM STILLS For bacanora, the still (called a tren) is often made from steel oil drums and repurposed water heaters augmented with copper pipes.

ALEMBIC STILLS In Oaxaca, the primary type of still for artisanal mezcal is the copper pot still known as an alambique, consisting of two parts. The first pot is usually set in concrete over an opening where a fire can be set. Above it is the 'hat' section, called the montera. Within this is a copper coil that exits the concrete tank near the base. These two sections are joined by a copper pipe, or elbow.

ABOVE: Loading a traditional copper still in San Dionisio Ocatepec, Oaxaca.

OPPOSITE: Tiny clay pot stills at the Ixcateco distillery in Santa María Ixcatlán, Oaxaca.

The first pot is where the distillation begins. It is loaded with fermented agave juice and fibres: the mash. Industrial methods have led to producers removing the fibres for efficiency and to protect the machinery. Artisanal and ancestral agave spirit-makers tend to keep the fibres in the mash, which they believe results in more complex flavours.

Fire below the pot heats the liquid within, causing the alcohol to evaporate. Vapours rise up through the first pot into the montera, connecting to the elbow. These vapours then flow along the hot pipe to the coil (serpentine) where they are condensed, returning to liquid form

CLAY POT STILLS Clay pot distillation is used in ancestral mezcal production, and consists of two superimposed clay pots. Fermented juice and fibre are added to the lower one. The second pot is mounted on top and has a sort of spoon suspended inside. Sometimes it is wooden, but it can simply be an agave leaf. At the top of the still there is a condenser made from copper or steel. The condenser is constantly cooled with cold water.

Each part of the still is sealed with a paste made from agave pulp or corn masa to stop vapours being lost during the process.

Once all the parts have been arranged, a fire is set beneath the lower pot (filled with the fermented agave). Once the alcohol reaches boiling point, it evaporates, passing through the second pot, where the steam collides with the condenser. Due to the change in temperature, the alcohol goes from gaseous to liquid, and the liquid in turn falls into the spoon. The spoon channels the liquid down a tube (usually made from bamboo-like carrizo) into a container, where it is collected.

REFRESCADERA In some communities they might team their distillation method with a refrescadera, a metal cylinder that sits around the bell-shaped part of the still and is continuously filled with cold water. These are commonly found in the regions of Miahuatlán and Ejutla in Oaxaca state. As the vapours rise up from the mash in the pot below, they recondense and fall back down. This means that the vapours have to work harder to get out of the pot, further refining what makes it through.

FILIPINO STILLS In the mountains, raicilla is usually distilled in copper alembic stills, while tabernas distilling raicilla near the coast usually employ the Filipino style, in which piece of hollowed-out trunk from the bonete tree sits atop a copper boiling pot. The vapours condense on the underside of the copper lid, before dripping onto a wooden spoon suspended within the still, which runs the distillate out of the tree trunk via a tightly bound agave leaf.

This method of distillation arrived on the coast of Jalisco when Filipino people sailed the Spanish trade route from Manila. These are portable stills and were originally used to make distillate from coconut, known as vino de coco.

BY-PRODUCTS After the first distillation there are two by-products: bagaso and vinaza. Bagaso, as previously mentioned, is the agave fibre waste. It is readily reused in the mezcal process, either in the next cook or in the agave fields as mulch, or for adobe blocks, paper and much more.

Vinaza is the liquid waste left in the bottom of the still after the first distillation. This comes out very acidic. In the history of very small productions, this was generally fed back into the earth. However, as production volume grew and there were more and more producers in mezcal producing areas, the vinaza has leached through the soil into the groundwaters and rivers, creating long-term environmental problems. Fortunately, efforts are being made to recycle the waste fibres and liquid.

ABOVE: *Cleaning the still at Mezcal Sombra in Matatlàn, Oaxaca.*

OPPOSITE: *A refrescadera at the Cuishe distillery near Miahuatlán, Oaxaca.*

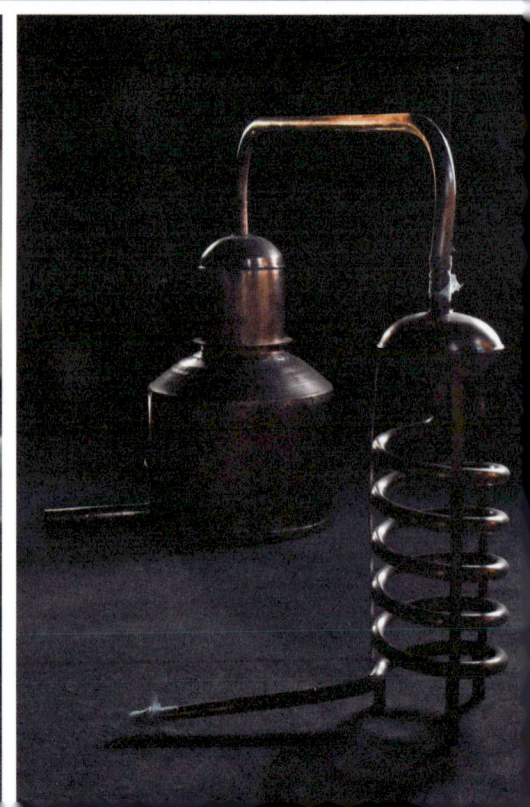

THE SECOND AND THIRD DISTILLATIONS The second round of

distillation should be done more slowly than the first. The copper stills
used for artisanal mezcal are relatively small compared to the modern
stills used for most spirit production. The elbow through which vapours
pass is low. If the still is run too hot and quickly, unwanted vapours and
impurities could also pass through and be condensed into the final liquid.

This second run of distillation is carefully monitored with a low,
consistent fire and can take up to 12 hours, more than double the time
for the first run. The liquid that comes out should not be gushing, or
even pouring. Usually, you can tell a second distillation by a slow drip,
sometimes guided by a string coming from the base of the condenser.

When the liquid is distilled the second time, the mezcal producer
divides it into what are known as 'cuts': heads, body and tails. The
heads, or puntas, come through first, and are the highest in alcohol,
usually 60–80%. This high-proof liquid can then be reused for cleaning
bottles, or even for starting the oven fire.

Second comes the sweet spot, the body, which is around 45–60%
alcohol. In Oaxaca, mezcal is typically drunk somewhere in this alcohol
range. Each producer will have their own methods and moments for
making cuts to best express the agave flavour and mouthfeel in their
final mezcal.

The rest of the liquid from the second distillation is the tails, which
can be as low as 16% alcohol. Occasionally tails are run through the still
again to extract every last drop of mezcal from the agave. The remaining
tails are dumped, or used for cleaning the palenque.

In some cases, producers will call for a triple distillation of their
mezcal. Some specific species need this based on their chemical makeup,
while some family traditions call for a third distillation to add further
qualities to a special batch.

Agave convallis (jabalí) is famous for needing at least three
distillations. During the fermentation, the mash tends to produce a lot
of foam, often spilling over the tinas. After
the second distillation, the liquid comes
out yellow. This is a visible sign that it has
too much methanol to be safe to drink.

A master mezcal producer can resolve
this in the third distillation. However,
with each distillation you lose quantity,

OPPOSITE, CLOCKWISE FROM TOP LEFT: *Removing agave
fibres after the first distillation run at a distillery
near Mitla, Oaxaca.*

*Apparatus of a typical copper alembic still in Oaxaca,
showing the montera on the pot and the coil.*

*The slow drip of mezcal into a cantera, a black pot
made from volcanic ash, at an ancestral distillery
in Santa Catarina Minas.*

so jabalí tends to be small batch, and correspondingly expensive. It is delicious, though, so well worth the effort put into making it.

When a producer is working on the final expression of their mezcal, they will taste the second distillation as it comes out of the still. They cross-reference the flavour with different points of alcohol percentage. The liquid comes out at a higher percentage to begin with, and gets lower as the liquid continues coming out of the still.

The traditional way to check the alcohol percentage is by looking at the perlas. These are bubbles that form on the surface of the distilled liquid after it has been dropped from a high point through the carrizo straw, called a venencia, into a wide-mouth cup, usually a jícara (gourd cup). The mezcalero can 'read' the perlas based on the size and duration of the bubbles.

When I first began drinking mezcal, people would shake the bottle to show that these bubbles formed, as a testament to quality. Although it doesn't quite signify quality, the perlas do form best when the mezcal is at its ABV sweet spot.

Producers can be extremely accurate using this rudimental technique. Once I visited Casa Palacios, home of Salvadores mezcal, where master mezcalero Flavio Pérez Méndez was trying the mezcal coming straight out of the still. Reading the perlas, he estimated the alcohol percentage at 50%. He tested the same sample with a modern alcohol metre, which read 49.5% – he was just half a percentage point out!

If the mezcalero particularly likes a certain percentage, for example 48.5%, they adjust the amount of body they collect to present at this percentage. The best sipping mezcals tend to be within that sweet spot, whether you are trying them on site at the palenque, in a bar or at home.

Espadín tends to be finished around 45%, while the wild agaves are collected at a higher cut of alcohol, usually 48% and above.

Sometimes a bit of the heads and tails are added into the final mezcal to adjust the alcohol percentage, taste and mouthfeel. This may happen to bulk out the final product. Ideally, this blending is minimal, as the point of making the cuts is to remove the methanol and other undesirables that exist in higher quantities in heads and tails.

You can tell a mezcal that has an excess of tails by a thinness to the mouthfeel; often there is acidity as well. If you drink mezcal with too much tails, it will definitely make you feel rough the next day. Mezcal with a lot of heads is – obviously – strong. It almost evaporates in the mouth, which can be delicious, but dangerously easy to drink!

As mezcal continues to be a bartender favourite, brands are looking to provide an appropriate choice for the cocktail station. It's not a great idea to sling cocktails with a base spirit at 50% – most cocktails use spirits at 40% or lower. Artisanal brands often use distilled water to reduce the percentage. Usually this happens only with espadín, as most producers prefer not to lose the hard-won sugars from wild agaves. Traditionalists frown on the use of water to lower the percentage, but in my opinion it is a healthier option than using tails.

BELOW LEFT: *Lorena Jiménez Sosa using a venencia to check the ABV of mezcal at the Jicarita palenque.*

BELOW RIGHT: *Perlas on the surface of freshly distilled mezcal.*

AGEING

Aged agave spirits are typically referred to as reposado (rested) or añejo (aged), depending on how long they have matured in oak barrels that have been charred (toasted) inside. Reposados are typically aged for six months, while añejos remain in the barrel for a year minimum.

Mexico has a long history of drinking agave spirits as blancos, meaning it is either completely unaged or rested in glass. Known as madurado (matured), resting in glass means the spirit is stored in glass vessels rather than plastic or wooden barrels, which lets the spirit breathe, and softens its texture. However, the popularity of barrel-aged spirits from Europe, as well as the transportation of tequila in barrels, has led to a tradition of ageing.

To make an aged tequila, or any spirit, you need a wooden barrel. Originally, spirits were stored in barrels for the sake of transportation. When the spirits took on properties from the wood, such as notes of oak, vanilla and caramel, these properties became sought after.

Ageing in the barrel is now an art form in itself. Distilleries such as La Tequileña (NOM 1146) have beautiful grand warehouses for ageing in barrels, experimenting with every kind of nuance they can draw from the agave spirit and wooden vessel. Different types of wood, such as French or American oak, pre-used barrels and different levels of char inside the barrel all influence the final taste.

If you visit, the team will show you the production step by step, past autoclaves the size of steam engines and huge stainless steel vats of fermenting agave. You can even step into a laboratory where they explain how they use their own stocks of differently aged spirits to blend for colour and flavour consistency.

Visiting the warehouse where tequila is aged is a special experience. Cool and peaceful, there is something transcendent about walking through stacks of wooden barrels, each taking their 'angels' share' of the spirit within.

Some sotoleros (makers of sotol, see page 171) will also age the spirit in wooden barrels, or make infusions with fruits and nuts or abocados (another spirit which is steeped with snakes, insects or herbs, often for a medicinal purpose). You can still find sotol infused with chuchupaxtle (a root used in herbal medicine).

OPPOSITE, CLOCKWISE FROM TOP LEFT: *A glass of unaged (blanco) tequila.*

Bottles of different expressions used to balance a batch of tequila.

A warehouse full of barrels ageing tequila.

A QUESTION OF SUSTAINABILITY

It is exciting to be part of the agave spirits boom, as more people around the world begin to enjoy these spirits, and to see producers getting recognition for their work. However, following the huge growth of the industry, how to sustain traditional practices and the environment are important topics of research and development.

When tequila's Denomination of Origin was established in 1974, production ramped up and many producers looked to make their process more efficient. They turned to industrial methods, such as the use of column stills and diffusers, and the speed at which agave can be processed with these techniques meant a much higher demand for the plants. Perhaps the most important factor about a diffuser is that it doesn't care about the ripeness of the plant: it can transform any type of agave starch into fermentable sugars. That means producers don't have to wait for agaves to become fully ripe.

Blue Weber became the only agave variety authorized for tequila production, leading to vast plantings of this particular type. These agaves were overharvested and underripe, so the final spirit gained from rushing the agave and the process doesn't have the rich, complex flavour and texture associated with traditional mezcals and tequilas. This leads to more brands relying on additives to reach the desirable flavour profile.

An extension of this issue is brands making agave spirits with unnaturally sweet profiles, which can be confusing for the consumer. When all you have tried are spirits with added sweeteners and glycerine, a traditional agave spirit can come as a bit of a surprise!

There are also dangers in relying on a monocrop, whether blue Weber or, more recently, espadín. In the late 1980s a collection of blights, fungi and pests called tristeza y muerte (sadness and death) wiped out thousands of acres of blue agave, bankrupting many tequila producers. Depending on a single agave species also limits the opportunity for variety and flavour. Would we choose only one grape variety for wine? The world of agave spirits is lucky to

OPPOSITE: *Wild agave in San Pedro Quiatoni, Oaxaca.*

BELOW: *A bat box (for pollination purposes) at the Proyecto LAM plant nursery.*

have a wealth of diverse plants, and each offers unique flavours in the final spirit. So why use only one type of agave?

Unfortunately, although mezcal has historically been made from a wealth of wild agaves, these plants are rare and laborious to harvest. As the industry booms, major brands are choosing to use only espadín, which is cheaper to produce. Nowadays, espadín fields in Oaxaca are becoming a monocrop, similar to what you find in Jalisco.

In Oaxaca, forests are being cut down to make way for the fields of domestic agave. As you drive into the mountains, the landscape becomes dominated by espadín. At first glance, it is beautiful, but the singularity of this plant, in place of the biodiverse forests, is a major concern. When you clear a landscape, it becomes vulnerable to erosion and water just runs off, stripping the soil further.

There was already an issue around the amount of wood being harvested and used to run the distilleries, with plans for certification that shows where the wood comes from and that it is sourced sustainably. But it is not yet effective. There are, however, producers and brands who are working to counter deforestation. Samuel Santiago Méndez, founder of Mezcal Los Ocotales, plants over 1,000 trees every year as reforestation helps replenish the water table. More trees help water percolate into the ground,

regenerating water security. The more time it takes for water to pass across a surface, the more likely the water will penetrate the soil.

Samuel is among a group of dedicated producers working to repopulate a range of endemic agaves into the hills around his town of San Dionisio Ocotepec. Projects like this, such as the work of Proyecto LAM in Santa Catarina Minas, are becoming more common. These actions will help support the diversity of pollinators, as well as preserving the unique agaves we currently have the luxury of accessing, for the future of agave spirits.

There is no single easy answer to the issue of sustainability when the demand for agave spirits is so high. We can invest in brands that have a clear origin story, are producer-owned or showcase their producers. We can support brands that engage with projects such as seed banks and growing programmes, water security and education initiatives. It is important that everyone takes accountability, from producer, brand and distributor to the consumer. By understanding the chain of production from agave to glass, we can encourage transparency in the industry.

Transparency in labelling and marketing helps enthusiasts to discern the origins of their favourite brands. Knowing the terroir is not just a matter of curiosity; it's an assurance of quality and a connection to the land. By celebrating and preserving the terroir, distilleries contribute to the preservation of their unique environments.

The identity of agave spirits needs to shift from cheap tequila shots to a more knowledgeable approach akin to that around wine or whisky. This will help the industry overall and be reflected in the price. We should consider what the brand is presenting, and drink with intention.

SECTION II:

SPIRIT PROFILES

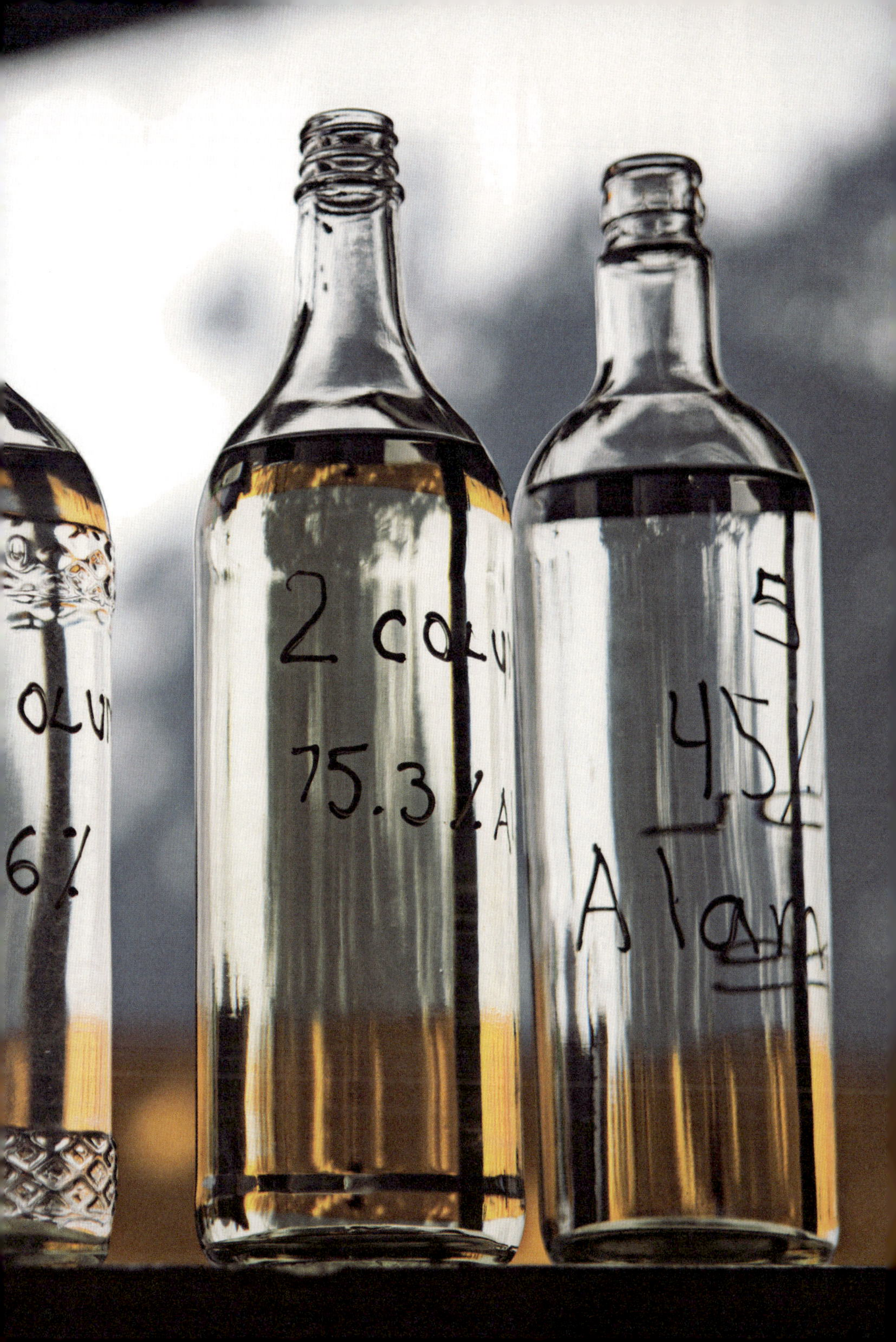
2 colu
75.3% A
5
45%
Alam

PULQUE

Pulque, although teqhnically not a spirit as it is fermented but not distilled, is included here first as the original agave drink. The pulquero plant (*Agave salmiana*) can take up to 16 years to produce aguamiel, the sap, which is then fermented. Pulque farmers, called tlachiqueros, usually have fields of plants that mature at slight intervals. Once the agave plant reaches maturity and starts growing its quiote (the point at which it would be cut if it were to be made into mezcal), the tlachiquero will use ropes made from agave fibre to tie back the agave's huge leaves in order to access the heart of the growing plant.

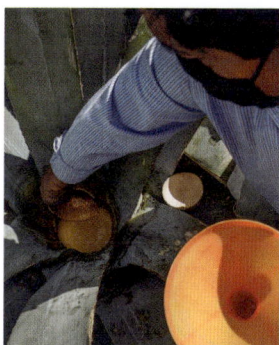

ABOVE: *Tlachiquero Felix Hernández harvesting aguamiel from a pulquero agave.*

OPPOSITE: *Mezcalero Pedro Martínez Jiménez with a pulquero agave.*

The quiote is then cut away and a bowl shape is scraped deep into the heart of the piña, which will hijack the sugars that would otherwise be used to fuel flower creation. This 'injury' causes the agave to produce the sap (aguamiel).

After a few days, aguamiel naturally begins to fill the bowl. In fact, the plants produce up to 5 litres (9 pints) per plant each dawn and dusk. This continues for several months, depending on the size of the original plant. The heart of a mature pulquero can weigh over 300 kilograms (660 pounds).

When aguamiel is drunk straight from the heart of the agave plant, the liquid is slightly yellow and translucent, tasting sweet and slightly yeasty. Between morning and evening harvests, the tlachiquero will make a lid for the bowl in the heart of the agave using one of the pulquero plant's thick, leathery leaves. This is to keep out bees and other insects, which are attracted to the sugary sap.

Once the aguamiel is harvested, fermentation happens so quickly that it reaches a low alcohol content in a matter of hours. It becomes white and lightly effervescent, tasting a bit like kombucha or rough cider. At this point it can be called pulque. Pulque can be made in any state as it is not defined by a DO. It is particularly popular in Estado de Mexico, Puebla and Hidalgo.

DRINKING PULQUE

In Mesoamerican society, pulque was considered a beverage of the gods. The most revered of these deities was Tepoztecatl, the god of pulque and fertility. Pulque was a ritual drink, and only priests, elders or warriors were permitted to consume it. In 1969 an 1,800-year-old mural was discovered at the Cholula archaeological site in the central highlands of Mexico. The painting shows the first visual record of the consumption of pulque.

Nowadays, pulque is usually drunk in designated bars called pulquerías. It is typically drunk out of a gourd called a jícara, or from tankards. In pulquerías you'll see images of Tepoztecatl and Mayahuel, a goddess of the agave plant, who is said to have 400 breasts (perhaps corresponding to the many spikes of an agave).

My regular pulquería is El Pulquito (The Little Pulque) in the famous mezcal-producing town of Santiago Matatlán, about an hour from Oaxaca City. It is run by Felix Hernández and his family, who have been tlachiqueros for five generations. Their pulque is fermented for a maximum of four days, getting a little tarter and a bit higher in alcohol with each passing day.

Felix describes how in some communities, midwives recommend pulque to breastfeeding women to increase breast milk production. Aguamiel and pulque are considered medicinal due to their range of vitamins, proteins and carbohydrates. Pulque is said to relieve gastrointestinal issues, stimulate appetite and combat weakness.

ABOVE: *Felix Hernández sharing some fresh aguamiel.*

Pulque can be drunk pure or as a curado, which is sweetened with fruits and syrups. This is popular in Mexico City, where the pulque is usually older and has a thick, slimy texture, which is definitely an acquired taste.

The rapid fermentation is responsible for two fundamental characteristics of pulque: the best stuff is fresh, and it doesn't travel well. There have

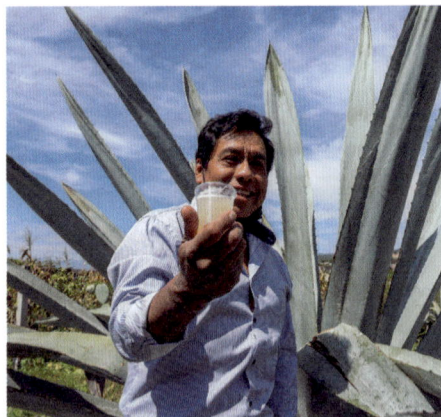

been attempts to preserve the ephemeral fermented flavour of pulque by bottling, canning and even distilling. One brand that has succeeded in bringing this drink to the market is Pulque Pachita.

COMITECO

A regional, contemporary type of distilled aguamiel is the spirit comiteco, which is produced in the southern state of Chiapas, Mexico. Some call it the missing link between pulque and mezcal. However, there are considerable differences. To produce comiteco, only the aguamiel is harvested, rather than the whole heart. There is no roasting of the agave, so no smoky flavour. The aguamiel is fermented for four to five days, and may also be mixed with piloncillo (unrefined sugar) wrapped in corn husks. The fermented mixture is then distilled twice, in a similar way to mezcal. Comiteco is then usually aged in glass bottles for about six months. The final spirit is herbaceous and earthy.

Brands of comiteco on the market that I recommend include: Balam, Nueve (9) Guardianes, Corazon Comiteco, Nueve (9) Estrellas.

PULQUE & COMITECO
BRAND DIRECTORY

PULQUE PACHITA

$$

One of the first successful brands of pulque on the market. David Castillo from Oaxaca's In Situ Mezcalería describes this drink as sweet, spicy, earthy and semi-bitter, the flavour of a lightly fermented pulque from the highlands of Mexico.

BALAM COMITECO

$$

Launched in 2016 by Xavier Villagrán as part of a range including sotol and raicilla. The brand's small batches of clay pot distilled comiteco are produced by maestro Enrique Dias in Chiapas. Musty on the nose, it is herbaceous, piney and a little zesty with further musty notes on the palate.

MEZCAL

OAXACA AND BEYOND

Famous for its mezcal production, Oaxaca state is a diverse terroir made up of over 150 species of agave, uniquely evolved to survive in each area. Near the capital city of Oaxaca de Juárez is a rich valley where espadín flourishes as far as the eye can see. There is also a high desert with forests of *Agave karwinskii* varieties. In the spring you can see pops of yellow where tepeztate are blooming on distant cliff faces. Beyond the mountains, the landscape becomes tropical, flourishing into coffee and banana groves.

This geographically diverse state also has many disparate communities who have evolved their own methods and styles of mezcal production that create a world of flavours in the final spirit. Many of these people don't speak Spanish as their first language; instead they speak one of a number of indigenous languages. Of these languages, Zapotec is prevalent, spoken by communities along the 'ruta de mezcal', which runs southeast from Oaxaca city all the way to the coast.

OPPOSITE: *Workers at the Son de La Luna palenque wearing masks while loading agave into the oven. These masks represent wild animals that accompany the 'old people' in costume on the Day of the Dead.*

RIGHT: *Tending to copper alembic stills at a large distillery in San Dionisio Ocotepec, Oaxaca.*

There isn't really such a thing as Oaxacan-style mezcal. Different areas have different native agaves, and their own traditions, techniques and equipment. While some of these practices are specific to Oaxaca, no single style represents the state's mezcal overall.

It is common for producers to make batches for various brands, and also for brands to work with several different producers, especially when palenques are small and not set up for large-scale mezcal production.

Beyond Oaxaca, there are nine other states within the DO for mezcal: Guerrero, San Luis Potosí, Zacatecas, Durango, Tamaulipas, Guanajuato, Puebla, Michoacán and Sinaloa. These regions have rich traditions of making agave spirits, with unique terroirs and methods of production. Michoacán in particular is a beautiful place, quite magical when you witness the migration of monarch butterflies, a flash of orange navigating the dense green mountain forests. With a wealth of wild agave plants, it is also the home of some fascinating mezcal (see pages 116–25).

ARTISANAL MEZCAL

When most people think of agave spirits, the artisanal style of mezcal is what comes to mind. It is the broadest category you will find in bars and liquor stores. There are hundreds of artisanal producers in Oaxaca state alone, each with their own particularities that contribute to the final nuances in the mezcal. The artisanal style is also typical of other mezcal-producing regions, such as the neighbouring states of Guerrero and Puebla.

While ancestral mezcal distillation (see page 76) has contested origins, the copper stills used for artisanal mezcal are known to have arrived with the Spanish in the 16th century. These stills are more efficient than clay pots, but less efficient than stainless steel column stills. However, there is an argument for the use of copper, as it helps remove sulphur from spirits.

According to the regulation NOM 70, which defines the certification for DO mezcal, artisanal mezcal should be made from 100 per cent mature agave, grown in regions protected by the DO for mezcal. Unlike ancestral production, most artisanal mezcal is made from cultivated espadín agave.

OPPOSITE, TOP: *La Jicarita palenque.*

OPPOSITE, BOTTOM: *Distilling at the palenque of Juan Antonio Coronel Maya in Nochixtlán, Oaxaca.*

ANCESTRAL MEZCAL

There is a particular group of mezcal fans obsessed with finding the funkiest sips and the most rustic styles of production. I am quick to point out that although these qualities are great as part of the complexity that makes up agave spirits, rustic or funky doesn't equal better. However, I am also enamoured with this style of mezcal, which usually falls into the ancestral category. 'Ancestral' was a term codified in a 2016 update of regulations governing mezcal, the NOM 70. These regulations specify that ancestral agave production must include the following elements: the agave hearts must be roasted in an underground stone oven, then crushed either by hand with a tahona, or a Chilean or Egyptian mill (mezcaleros often use a wood chipper as well), then fermented along with agave fibres in stone, earth, wood, clay or animal skins. Finally, distillation must take place with direct fire using a clay pot still, and agave fibres must be included.

A very small number of the distilleries in Mexico, mostly in Oaxaca, produce ancestral mezcal. They share a minerality that comes from the distillation, as well as unexpectedly lactic notes that come from ageing cooked agave and slow fermentation.

Visiting an ancestral palenque is an unforgettable experience, especially if you get to see some of the intricate processes. Every step, from roasting to fermenting to distilling, is done by hand, and each step is an intimate dance between tradition, craftsmanship and passion. It is produced in the tiniest of batches, often no more than a few hundred litres at a time. This rarity is part of its magic.

Anthony Ayon, founder of Autora Mezcal, remembers meeting their producer Rolando Ángeles for the first time: 'This was mezcal crafted with an ancient soul, and Rolando personally oversaw every detail of the process. He is a master mezcalero in the truest sense of the word, with calloused hands and a heart deeply connected to the land and the agave plants he tends. Sipping one of his mezcals feels like discovering a hidden treasure that few outside the local pueblos ever get to experience.'

The small batches are almost at the scale of what might be produced in a kitchen pan. During the period of prohibition in Mexico that supressed agave spirits production (early 17th–late 18th century), these materials and scale made it easy to take this style underground. If the authorities showed up, the makers could claim they were cooking pots.

OPPOSITE: *Sósima Olivera Aguilar stoking the fire beneath clay pot stills in Sola de Vega, Oaxaca.*

BELOW: *Clay pot stills at the Ixcateco palenque in Santa María Ixcatlán, Oaxaca.*

The term 'ancestral' suggests that this style of spirit was made and sipped by mezcaleros from pre-conquest generations – Mesoamerican ancestors of the modern-day mezcal producer. Although this notion is romantic, it is frequently contested. Sceptics are convinced that distillation arrived with the conquistadors (see page 16). Regardless of the exact date of the beginning of mezcal production, and whether or not clay pots were used for distillation, we know that people have been making clay pots in the town of Santa María Atzompa, Oaxaca, since it was founded in the 7th century.

INDUSTRIALIZING MEZCAL

As mezcal reaches a wider global audience, there is ever-building pressure for the industry to expand and industrialize. There are some obvious lessons to be learned from the rapid industrialization of tequila, and unsustainable growth is a concern for mezcal too.

There are some factors in place that help check the rise of industrial processes, such as the certification of artisanal practices. Not all mezcal brands use the labels 'artisanal' or 'ancestral'; they often just state 'mezcal' on the label. This is due to steps in their production process falling outside the guidelines for those certifications, as defined by the regulatory board. The guidelines are meant to protect small-batch traditional mezcal.

For a long time, I made the jump to describe all of these other brands as 'industrial'. This was largely due to my experience with the mezcal available at Mexico City airport, which consisted of a few brash-looking brands with a low price tag and low alcohol content (by mezcal standards). However, 'industrial' isn't a term used officially. These brands are just mezcal without the prefix of artisanal.

As a rule, a great sipping mezcal is over 45% ABV. Even for cocktails, I wouldn't go lower than 40%, as there will be at the very least a lot of water diluting it, if not other, less desirable, additions. I would still avoid a brand with a price too good to be true.

OPPOSITE: *Taking cooked agave out of the autoclave at the Scorpion mezcal distillery in Oaxaca.*

To achieve a low-cost mezcal, brands usually need to produce their liquid in large volumes, quickly and efficiently. They also lean towards homogeneity to meet supermarket standards and fit neatly into cocktail recipes. These requirements don't come naturally to agave spirits. Larger, more industrial distilleries speed up production by employing industrial methods developed by tequila producers. These include autoclaves instead of ovens, stainless steel vats for fermenting, column stills and diffusers. This equipment can make a huge impact on the volume of spirit that can be produced in a fraction of the traditional time.

As well as prohibiting the use of these methods, the certification is also supposed to prohibit mixtos and the use of cane distillates, and yet there are numerous tales of huachicoleros (the name given to someone who illegally sells gasoline or adulterated alcohol) selling truckloads of cane distillate to producers across regions to meet volume demand. Mixtos are agave spirits made with raw sugars other than agave, such as sugar cane. Mixto tequilas are permitted.

Like most issues relating to mezcal, things aren't straightforward. There are strict rules for mezcal to reach certified artisanal status, such as not using an autoclave or adding artificial yeasts. However, evidence of excess product in the market due to unregulated sugar cane or other additives is rife. Not all mezcals outside the artisanal and ancestral categories are equal.

Since so much passion, history and effort goes into the production of agave spirits, and since a wealth of options is available on the shelf, it's a good idea to look for information about the materials and tools used in production, rather than going straight for bottles labelled 'artisanal'. I always question labels that are light on detail.

OPPOSITE, CLOCKWISE FROM TOP LEFT: *Within the autoclave, looking out.*

Shredded cooked agave.

One of the machines used for breaking down cooked agave and separating juice from fibre.

PECHUGA

As if agave spirits didn't have enough variety already, you then have pechuga. Pechuga means 'breast' in Spanish, and it gets its name from the tradition of suspending meat (usually a turkey or chicken breast) in the still during distillation. It is typically made with espadín agave, as this is the most cost-effective.

Pechuga-style mezcals are usually triple-distilled, with additional ingredients, such as fruits, nuts and spices, added to the distillation. These ingredients add rich flavours to the final product, while the meat itself contributes to a silky-smooth mouthfeel. The meat does not touch the liquid, but is suspended in the top of the still, acting as a filter for oils that may burn off from the additional ingredients.

Sometimes the extra ingredients are suspended in a basket, and other times the mezcalero will add them straight into the pot of the

still with the previously distilled liquid. As the mezcal distils for a third time, vapours pass through the meat, which absorbs the flavours of the ingredients. The meat cooks in the distilling vapours, releasing proteins and collagen that contribute to the texture. There is also a style of sotol similar to Oaxacan pechuga called carne (meat). Rather than using a chicken or a turkey breast, this is usually made with venison.

Pechuga is often made during the harvest season. Some producers wait until after Day of the Dead in November, using elements from the altar to make the pechuga, which is then drunk over Christmas and New Year. Whenever the pechuga is made, the ingredients vary greatly depending on the family recipe. Symbolically, the use of the meat is as a sacrifice and an offering, which relates this practice back to pre-Hispanic times, when sacrifices were made to give thanks. It is quite a recent development for outsiders to have access to these pechugas, as they were typically saved for family consumption.

BELOW: *Juan Carlos González Díaz and his wife preparing the ingredients to make a traditional pechuga-style mezcal at their palenque in Mitla, Oaxaca. While he is hanging the raw turkey in the montera part of the still, she is preparing the fruits, nuts and spices to go into the liquid.*

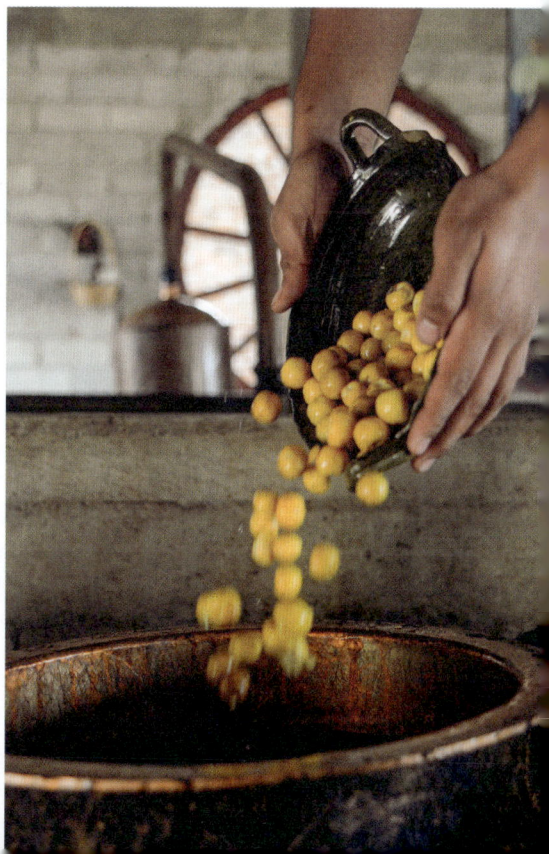

PECHUGA PRODUCERS

Although pechugas are still relatively rare outside Oaxaca, there are a few producers who have brought them to the international market. These include Casa Cortés, La Jicarita, Gracias a Dios and Del Maguey. The last two brands have taken things even further, using different kinds of meats.

Mezcal Del Maguey makes a pechuga using Ibérico ham as a replacement for the poultry breast. Unlike most pechugas, the flavour of the ham in Del Maguey's experiment actually does come through. It's well balanced, layering some salty, savoury notes into the mezcal. Another producer I have visited tried using thick-cut bacon. This wasn't quite so successful, as the fat from the meat dripped into the liquid, making the final product strangely oily, although admittedly the flavour was quite fun.

La Jicarita, made by maestro Celso Martínez López, is what I would describe as a 'classic' pechuga. Celso suspends a turkey breast in his still and then adds the pechuga ingredients straight to the still. Although he keeps the exact recipe close to his chest, orange and pineapple come through clearly in the final drink. Celso also experiments with what some might call 'vegan' pechuga, or mezcal destilado con (distilled with). As you might have guessed, this is agave distilled with other things, but not meat. I met him while documenting the process for another brand he produces for, Dangerous Don. Their flagship product is his espadín distilled with coffee. Elegant and aromatic, this mezcal is a perfect digestif, and also gives a great hit of flavour in a Negroni.

Another destilado con that goes very well in a Negroni is the espadín with mole negro (also known as Oaxacan mole). Mole is a rich sauce made with over thirty ingredients, including fruits, spices, nuts, seeds, charred tortillas and – famously – cacao. These elements are crushed into a paste and then mixed with stock. Mole is typically served at celebrations such as baptisms and weddings, for which huge pots are made to feed hundreds of guests. To use mole for destilado con, the mezcalero usually adds the paste straight into the still with the previously twice-distilled mezcal. Brands that have brought a mezcal con mole to the market include Quiquiriqui, Palomo and Salvadores.

If you can't get your hands on one of these, mole bitters are also a bartender favourite to add some body to a Mexican-inspired cocktail (see pages 200–13).

Other exciting destilado con mezcals that are arriving on the market include Celso's Cempasuchil (marigold), which is a winner with bartenders; José Santiago López's distillate with fresh tobacco leaves which Noble Coyote are bottling with him; and the Salvadores mezcal distilled with roasted corn.

These destilados can be polarizing among the agave spirits community. Some consider them untraditional, and that they are an unnecessary layer of flavour to a drink that is already complex. However, the other side of the coin is that these are playful creations that can offer complementary notes to the agave spirit.

BELOW LEFT: *Stoking the fire while distilling at the Corte Vetusto palenque.*

BELOW RIGHT: *A huge pot of mole negro made for the wedding of mezcalera Lidia Hernández, who produces Mezcal Desde la Eternidad.*

PRODUCER STORIES

CONEJO

Antonio Carlos Martínez, known to his friends as Conejo (rabbit), is a third-generation mezcalero from Minas. He is generous and welcoming. When I think of ancestral mezcal, it is usually Conejo's that comes to mind. He usually serves it in a jícara, or dried gourd. Considering these slightly porous vessels 'share' your mezcal with you, it's lucky that jícaras are less shot-sized than a bowl the size of your face!

The mezcals are particularly potent and speak to the clay pot style in taste. Perhaps the intensity comes from the amount of time he leaves his agave between cooking and crushing, during which a moho covers the agave, or the fact that he has long fermentation times of up to two weeks. He once told me the way he knows his ferment is ready for distillation is that the vinegary taste makes him gag!

Although they sound strange, these slow steps in the process add flavour, often on the spectrum of cheesy (lactic), mineral and nutty. It's one of the things I love most about agave spirits; depending on the particular style of the producer, you can be sipping a clean, pure spirit, yet find the wildest and funkiest of flavours.

Conejo's mezcal is not widely available beyond his tasting room. If you are lucky, you may find some bottles through a mezcal club such as Maguey Melate, run by Dalton Kreiss. Maguey Melate (muh-gay may lah-tay) translates literally to 'agave makes my heart beat'.

Maguey Melate uses its active club membership to help consumers discover the origins of mezcal beyond the big brands. Their mezcal is packaged as an educational experience, resembling a suitcase filled with mezcal samples, information cards and images about the featured producer.

OPPOSITE: *Antonio Carlos Martínez going through an order of mezcal in the tasting room at his palenque in Santa Catarina Minas, Oaxaca.*

RECOMMENDED CONEJO MEZCAL

Maguey Melate by Antonio Carlos Martínez
46.7% ABV
Notes: wet earth, red dry fruits, floral

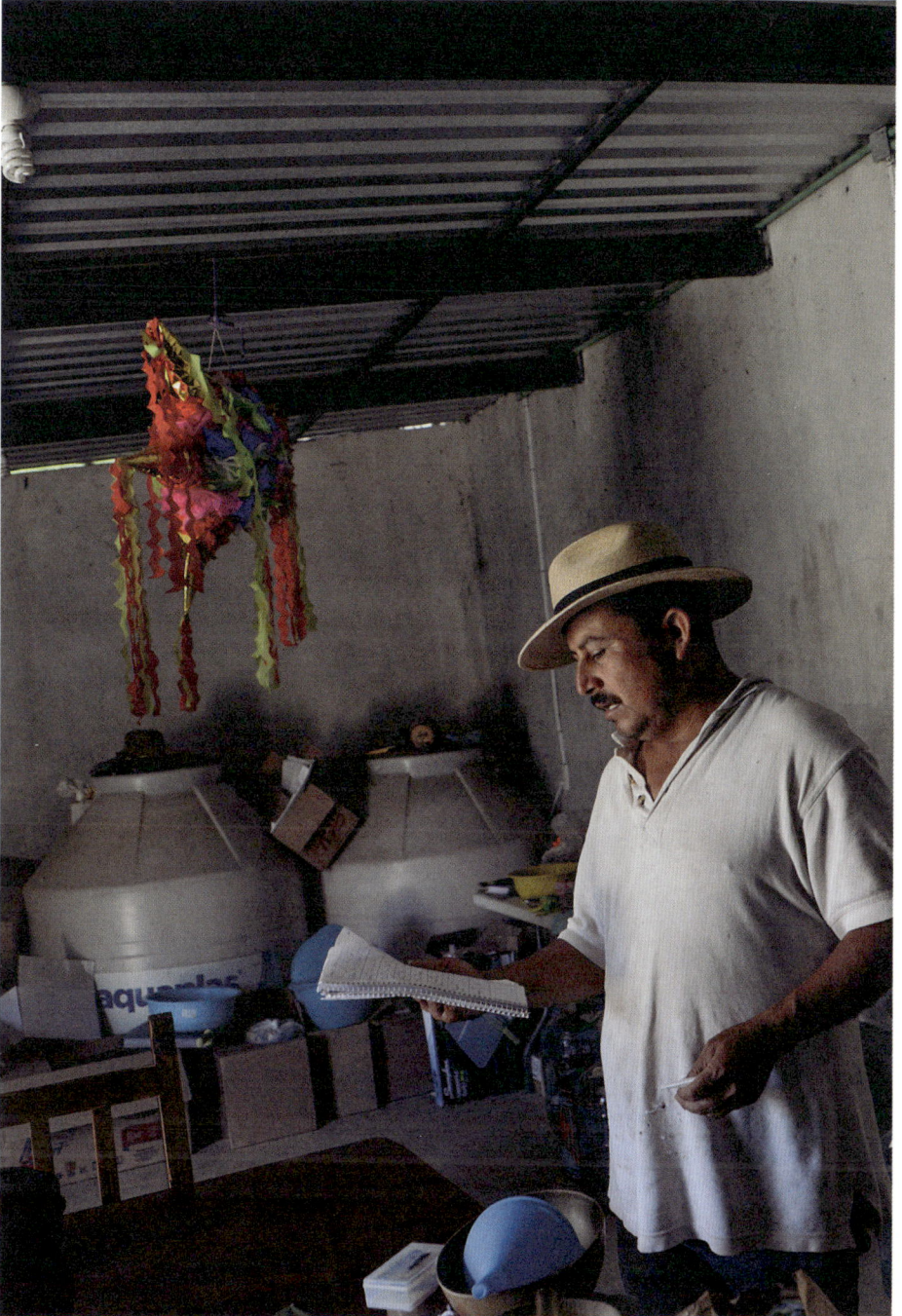

IXCATECO

One of the most beautiful and extreme examples of the ancestral style that I have visited is in the village of Santa María Ixcatlán in the Mixteca region of Oaxaca. My earliest visits to Ixcatlán included getting lost, multiple flat tyres from driving across the cliff-like terrain, and the laborious process of coaxing a herd of donkeys off the only path.

Fortunately, driving off the highway into the mountains is always worth it, and this region feels quite surreal. Shouldering the biosphere between Oaxaca and Puebla, the huge agaves emerge dinosaur-like from the landscape in the misty forest. *Agave papalome* is the species most associated with this region, although there are likely to be many unregistered agave species here.

Amando Alvarado Álvarez and his family produce a brand of mezcal called Ixcateco, which is also the name of their community's language. They are Xuani people, and as well as using profits from their sales to preserve this Mesoamerican language, they are committed to producing tiny-batch ancestral mezcal.

OPPOSITE, TOP LEFT: *Mezcalero Amando Alvarado Álvarez.*

OPPOSITE, TOP RIGHT: *The Ixcateco palenque sits a little down the mountain from the town of Santa María Ixcatlán, Oaxaca. You can just make out the cowhide fermentation vats in the entrance.*

BELOW: *Clay pot distillation in the Ixcateco palenque.*

RECOMMENDED IXCATECO MEZCALS

Papalome
46.1% ABV
Notes: smoke, spice, earth, mineral, dark chocolate

Ticunchi 750
46.1% ABV
Notes: candyfloss (cotton candy), lactic, damp cardboard

After arriving in Ixcatlán, we followed Amando beyond the town and down the other side of the mountain, until we saw a plume of smoke emerging from a thatched roof. The smoke came from a set of tiny clay pot stills running inside. Unfortunately, this smoke has set fire to the thatch – more than once.

To the side is a pit oven that can hold around 2 tonnes of raw agave. The hole is small enough that the family uses palm leaves from around the palenque, rather than tarps or sacking, to cover it during cooking. Once the agave are cooked, they are crushed by hand using wooden clubs before the mash is ready to ferment.

Although the clay pot is typically the key feature of ancestral mezcal, in this instance it is the fermentation that captures people's imagination. The cooked agave liquid is suspended in hammocks made from cowhide. If you place your hand on the bulging hide, it feels warm from the active ferment. It feels alive.

Mezcal Ixcateco, made by the Amando's family, is as rustic as it comes. It is savoury and earthy, reminiscent of the processes that formed it. Like all agave spirits, it should be drunk with a reverence to the work and history behind it.

Amando emphasizes that when you buy his family's mezcal you are trading two things: money and culture. 'Many things that we make, such as agave spirits, have a deep, symbolic meaning. We would like to involve you in our life and customs so that you will enjoy our agave spirit responsibly.'

REAL MINERO

My first visit to Santa Catarina Minas, Oaxaca, was in May 2014, to meet legendary producer Graciela Ángeles Carreño. Described as a woman 'born between agaves', she runs Real Minero with her siblings. While Graciela manages the administrative side, her brother Edgar watches over the physical side of production.

After harvesting the agave, it is brought to the palenque, which opens onto a warehouse-like space with two pit ovens. Once the agave is cooked, they bring it inside, where they rest it. Graciela trims the cooked agave of excess moho before crushing it, which could be done by hand or using a shredding machine. This detail of the process is distinguished on the labels.

The fermentation is done in wooden tinas. Although it is open fermentation, they use petates (woven palm mats) over the top to regulate the heat. Each tina has a name, such as el gatito (the kitten) and la guerra (war), which speaks to the unique personality of flavour that develops during fermentation.

The distillation is done in clay pots, as is the ancestral tradition in Santa Catarina Minas. There is a large space neatly laid out with clay stills. It definitely looks grander and more efficient than the typical pot set-up you see in the area.

Graciela describes how 'when a mezcal is distilled in clay, more flavours are condensed'. She says that consumers have been surprised at how bold the flavours can be, and how finessed the spirit is considering the 'rudimentary nature of the system'. They don't stay with the clay pot tradition because it's especially lucrative, or easier. 'It's how our fathers and grandfathers did it, and how we want our children to do it.'

Real Minero was founded by Graciela's father, Lorenzo Ángeles Mendoza, in 1978, and is credited as the oldest in Santa Catarina Minas. The family's roots are in local history, as is their dedication to traditional practices. These elements inspired the Real Minero motto, 'Porque sólo lo auténtico perdura' (Because only the authentic lasts).

OPPOSITE, TOP: *Graciela Ángeles Carreño.*

OPPOSITE, BOTTOM: *Loading the oven with trunk-like hearts of* Agave karwinskii *at the Real Minero palenque.*

RECOMMENDED REAL MINERO MEZCALS

Tequilana	**Largo**	**Arroqueño**
53.4% ABV	49.6% ABV	52.6% ABV
Notes: earth, pepper, chocolate, tomato	Notes: pepper, coconut, nuts	Notes: earth, citrus, herbs, sweet

In 2019, Graciela and the Real Minero team opened Proyecto LAM, named in honour of Don Lorenzo. Proyecto LAM was founded with the aim of studying agave and its pollinators. Many of the plants began their life while Don Lorenzo Ángeles was still alive, well before the study of rare agave plants. Now the Ángeles family carefully detail what happens to each plant, which can be seen on the meticulous labels. Each year they produce a special edition of Real Minero to fund the work at Proyecto LAM.

Visiting the site of Proyecto LAM is captivating. It is a wondrous garden, bursting at the seams with all kinds of agave — a must-have experience for anyone exploring the world behind mezcal. They also have a bar on site, where you can try different expressions of the Real Minero brand. There are too many to list, and many are limited editions. But if you have the chance, I would highly recommend their distillate of *Agave tequilana*.

Despite being at the luxury end of the price range for agave spirits, the brand has long been a favourite of international bartenders. The bottle is understated, using bands of colour to distinguish between agave expressions. The agave shines through its distillation, showcasing herbaceous, occasionally spicy notes. Unlike some mezcals from Minas, lactic notes are minimal, but the spirits do show minerality.

RAMBHÁ

Mezcal Rambhá is produced by mezcalera Rosario Ángeles Vázquez on the outskirts of Santa Catarina Minas, Oaxaca. Rosario comes from a family of tomato farmers and previously taught English. Her decision, in spring 2020, to pivot and make mezcal raised more than a few eyebrows. But she has taken the challenge in her stride. The talent and perseverance she brings to the mezcal industry is inspiring.

The Rambhá palenque is still aesthetically rustic, with carrizo (woven reed) walls. There is a pit oven outside, while inside are wooden fermentation vats and two clay pot stills. Rosario can normally be found trimming cooked agave ready to hand-crush. There are always animals around: a cat, dogs, a flock of chickens and turkeys, and donkeys in the next-door field. Her daughter even had a pet piglet, an entertaining addition to the menagerie.

Despite this, the palenque is one of the most peaceful I have ever visited. Wide-open views stretch past fields of flowers and agave to distant mountains. Rosario invites visitors to the palenque to a stellar tasting. She offers expressions ranging from espadín, tobalá, tobasiche and tepeztate to a vibrant pechuga. Tobasiche is usually my go-to. This agave is endemic to Santa Catarina Minas, and Rosario shares an elegant expression of it.

Rosario has also stepped away from the classic flavours you find in Santa Catarina Minas, making a mezcal distilled with other elements, such as chocolate. Her version of this has beautiful light aromas of cacao, vanilla and Oaxacan spices. She made a name for herself in the industry with a pechuga-style mezcal using lobster!

The image on the label, which shows an apparently naked woman and an agave plant, could easily be interpreted as the goddess Mayahuel. However, not coming from a mezcal-producing family, Rosario wanted to add her own voice to the conversation. She explains that the image and the name Rambhá allude to a Hindu goddess of love and pleasure.

OPPOSITE, CLOCKWISE FROM TOP LEFT:
Rosario Ángeles Vásquez checking the perlas.

A tasting of Rambhá at the palenque.

Rosario emptying the clay pot stills.

RECOMMENDED RAMBHÁ MEZCALS

Espadín – Tepeztate	Tobasiche	Chocolate
49% ABV	50% ABV	58% ABV
Notes: smoke, herbs, earth	Notes: citrus, herbs, floral, smoke	Notes: cacao, vanilla, chocolate, cinnamon

AUGURIO

Augurio is a young brand developed by sisters Araceli and Berenice Rodríguez. Both sisters remember being intrigued by the mezcal process when they were children. Despite raised eyebrows about whether it was appropriate for the girls to be helping with production, their father Vincente encouraged their interest.

The sisters chose to start their own palenque away from the family production, settling just off the highway beyond the town of Zaachila. While their father and uncles have typically worked in an artisanal style using a stone mill and copper stills, the sisters continue to forge their own path, choosing instead to hand-crush their agave with wooden mallets. They also experiment with clay pots. Araceli told me that they were inspired by Rosario Ángeles Vásquez, the mezcalera behind Rambhá (see page 92). Not just by her process, but as an independent, first-generation mezcalera.

Berenice has a couple of reasons for choosing hand-crushing. In her opinion, crushing the agave using a wooden mallet helps open up the cooked agave fibres, allowing the natural yeasts to have more impact. This method also provides more employment, which gives the sisters a greater opportunity to hire locally and engage with the community.

As well as using some 'ancestral' techniques, the Augurio palenque also embraces modern technology. The use of wood and gas are concerns when considering sustainability in the production of agave spirits. This has led the sisters to install solar panels. Eventually, they anticipate running the distillery and adjacent bottling facility using only solar power. As well as the solar panels, they use other contemporary tools, such as pumps, to fill the still with shishe (the agave liquid after the first distillation) for the second round of distillation.

The sisters manage the production equally, with Berenice more focused on the physical process and Araceli managing the

OPPOSITE, TOP: *Sisters Araceli and Berenice Rodríguez standing with the mallets they use to hand crush cooked agave at their palenque in Zaachila.*

OPPOSITE, BOTTOM: *Berenice raises a copita of mezcal.*

RECOMMENDED AUGURIO MEZCALS

Espadín 41	Tepeztate	De Lumbre
41% ABV	46% ABV	45% ABV
Notes: cooked maguey, earth, citrus	Notes: wild flowers, cooked agave, intense wood	Notes: herbs, sweet fruits, sweet cooked agave, subtle anise

marketing of the brand. Having a sister myself, I was curious how they worked together. Although they laugh about the sisterly rows, Araceli said, 'We fight as equals. I love my sister a lot. It is complicated, but amazing. You find the patience.'

The sisters called the brand Augurio, meaning 'good omen,' based on stories they were told by their grandfather. The goddess Mayahuel influences people by using omens, or signs. The sisters explained that as they walk through the landscape, these omens guide their decisions on whether to cut an agave or leave it to flower. So when they were inspired to start a brand, they were very clear about it: 'It was an omen.'

The Augurio sisters want to be very clear about the make-up of the liquid. They are not looking for a rustic, smoky mezcal – instead, they present a botanic-forward profile. Araceli explains that they have 'inherited a recipe, but we have been polishing the details to give it our own identity'.

FANE KATSINI

Sola de Vega is a beautiful, luscious area in the Sierra Sur, about a three-hour winding drive from Oaxaca City. The area is best known as a hub for mezcal production, particularly using clay pot stills and tobalá agave. It is also common to find producers using canoas (hollowed-out tree trunks) for crushing and fermenting. Mezcals from this region have rich, lactic, sometimes nutty flavours.

I visited the area with Sósima Olivera Aguilar, who guided me through agave plantations and down to a river flanked by beautiful sabino trees. These trees are endemic to Sola, and are known locally as 'old men of the river' because of their huge, wrinkled buttresses. Thanks to its natural water-wicking properties, the wood from these trees was traditionally used for fermentation vats.

At the palenque, Sósima runs the show. She grabbed handfuls of fermenting agave fibres and held them up to her face, as a smile spread from ear to ear. Then, after stoking the fires, she went on to collect hot mezcal as the distillate dripped from the pots above.

Back in Oaxaca City, Sósima is a regular speaker at mezcal events, sharing her experiences and vision for the future. Her passion for generations of process is palpable. This, along with her enthusiasm, is what is going to be necessary for the tradition of clay pot mezcal production to survive.

Sósima works with a cooperative of producers called Tres Colibrí, and bottles her mezcal under the name Fane Kantsini, who was a legendary protector of the region. The label, which depicts a hummingbird, comes from an engraving made by the Oaxacan artist known as Bouler (see page 184).

As with many small-batch productions, especially those produced within a collective of producers, the stock varies. As well as growing tobalá and arroqueño, the collective grows also works with chato, pelón verde, barril, jabalí, coyote and sierra negra varieties. The availability of particular expressions depends on the season, creating distinct batches, or vintages, that are all unique.

OPPOSITE, TOP: *Sósima Olivera Aguilar in a field of espadín near the palenque in Sola de Vega.*

OPPOSITE, BOTTOM: *Sósima tending to the clay pot stills.*

RECOMMENDED FANE KATSINI MEZCALS

Chato	**Barril**	**Mexicanito**
50% ABV	50% ABV	50% ABV
Notes: mineral, saline	Notes: floral, mineral, earth	Notes: herbs, tropical

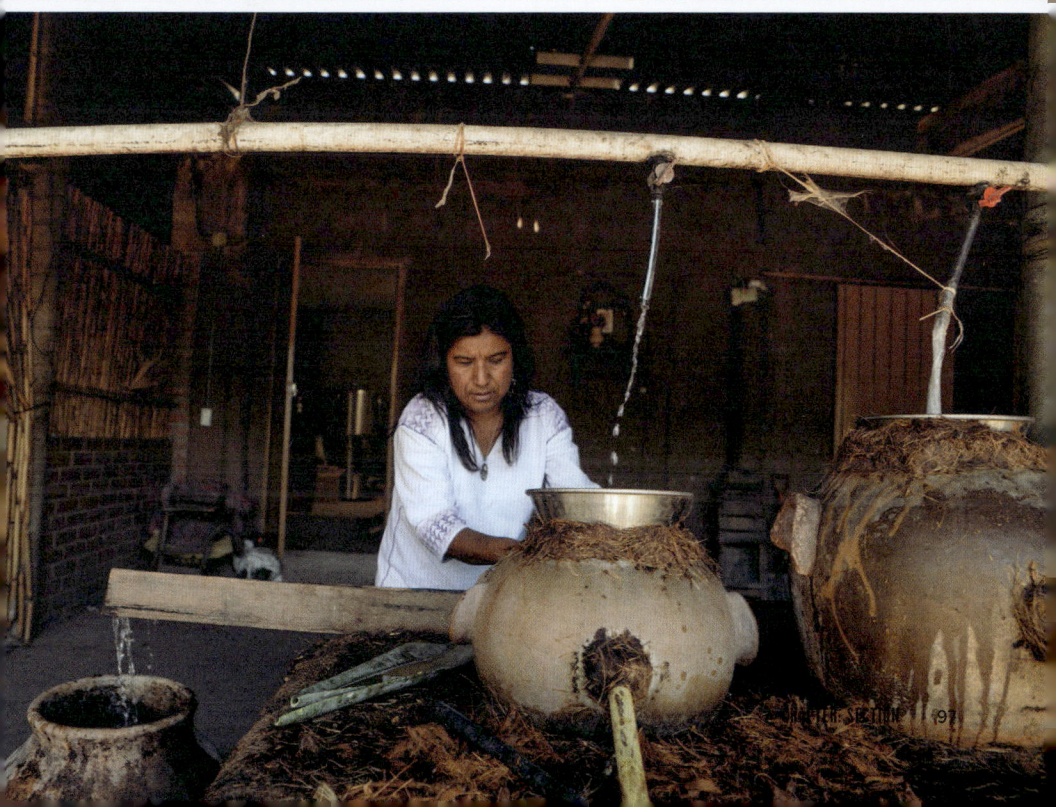

SIETE MISTERIOS

Siete Misterios is one of the best-known mezcals to have emerged from Sola de Vega. The brand was founded in 2008 by brothers Eduardo and Julio Mestre. They are pioneering in their efforts to bring clay pot mezcal to the international market, a style that makes up less than 1 per cent of total mezcal production.

The Siete Misterios palenque Rancho Concordia has all the elements you would expect to see at a mezcal producer in Sola de Vega: a pit oven, wooden fermentation vats and a series of small clay pot stills. There are, however, some innovations for efficiency and to help the team understand their results more clearly.

The oven is brick-lined to preserve heat. Mestre described how the tinas are a little bit shorter and wider in order to make it easier for the yeast to move around. The day-to-day running of the distillery is overseen by the brothers' mother, Ángeles, and her partner Eduardo Amador. They engage a collective of producers from the area. Originally, these producers would make limited-edition batches at their own palenques, but this led to challenges, especially in the consistency of yield. Now most producers work

OPPOSITE, TOP: *Separating the heads and tails while distilling.*

OPPOSITE, BOTTOM: *A clay pot still.*

BELOW LEFT: *A rock-lined pit oven at the Siete Misterios palenque.*

RECOMMENDED SIETE MISTERIOS MEZCALS

Tobalá	Doba-Yej	Pechuga
49.5% ABV	44% ABV	49% ABV
Notes: citrus, floral, earth, herbs, sweet agave	Notes: floral, citrus, caramel	Notes: fruit, spices, aromatic herbs

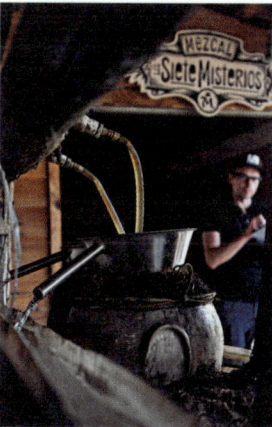

in the purpose-built Siete Misterios distillery. The site is a place to share knowledge and experience. While I visited, a young producer was running through a practice distillation, distilling colas from a previous batch, to get a better feel for the process.

Mestre explained to me: 'It's an alliance between the mezcaleros and us, which we pursue to learn the best practices from each mezcalero, then share with all the other mezcaleros we work with, not only the ones who produce in Rancho Concordia.'

As the Siete Misterios brand grew, they needed to expand, which was not possible to do with just a small-batch, clay pot, and specifically wild agave concept. This led to the copper-still expression, Doba-Yej, which means espadín in Zapotec. This is to distinguish it from the espadín they have in their original clay pot range. They work with three different producers from three different towns to produce the Doba-Yej: Santiago Matatlán, San Dionisio Ocotepec and San Carlos Yautepec.

Siete Misterios has an iconic aesthetic that connects their whole range of expressions. This is a skeletal family led by the character Porfirio, with drawings inspired by the etchings of 19th-century Mexican artist José Guadalupe Posada.

The Mestre brothers developed Siete Misterios to 'taste like the mezcal you drink in Oaxaca' – in other words, fresh from a palenque.

VIEJO INDECENTE

Miahuatlán is a particularly well-loved mezcal-producing region in Oaxaca. The area, sometimes referred to as 'tierra blancas' (white earth), has a unique soil type rich in calcium. It is drier than other mezcal-producing regions in Oaxaca, which makes the agaves work harder to survive by digging their roots down further into the earth to draw up more minerals while focusing their nutrients into their piña. This creates unusual depth and sweetness in the agave. According to Gabriel Pacheco, founder of Viejo Indecente, this terroir is very rare. It is dry but full of nutrients, perfect for agave.

Viejo Indecente is made by the Lucas family, whose family brand is 400 Lustros.

Unusually, they use a masonry oven for steam-cooking their agave. This is more typical in some of the older tequila productions. In this instance, the decision comes from a desire to make the process more sustainable. The main thing, Gabriel explains, is that by cooking the agave in this way, it steams consistently without charring. Steaming efficiently uses the entire plant, as burnt or charred pieces do not need to be removed. In traditional ovens a large percentage of the agave is charred, which translates into a compound called furfural when fermented. This is one of the undesirable elements that can come through in agave spirits and lead to a producer failing lab tests when trying to get certified. In addition, the oven is run with gas, rather than cut-down living trees. Distillation is conducted over a wood fire, but using only deadwood found on their property.

Due to the terroir where the Lucas family produce their mezcal, the spirit takes on strong mineral notes. Petrichor on the nose gives way to bright and well-defined agave flavours. The smoke is very light, considering it comes from the ambient smoke within the palenque, rather than from a pit-oven cook.

ABOVE: *José Lucas and his wife Clara, at their distillery in San Isidro Guishe, Oaxaca.*

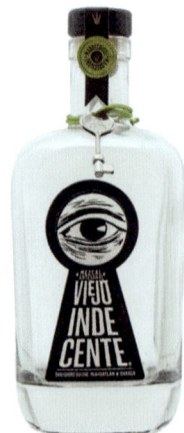

RECOMMENDED VIEJO INDECENTE MEZCALS

Madrecuishe	Espadín	Tepeztate
48% ABV	45% ABV	48% ABV
Notes: pepper, fruit, citrus spice, herbs, sweet	Notes: mineral, spices, salt, light herbs, caramelized agave	Notes: green peppers, salt, tomatoes, jalapeños

PENSADOR

BELOW: *Atenógenes and son, José García, at their distillery in San Isidro Guishe.*

Just along from the Lucas family in San Isidro is the calle Pensamiento, which leads to the palenque of Atenógenes and José García, the original producers of Pensador mezcal. Pensador was founded by Ben Schroder in 2015. These days, Ben still collaborates with José and Atenógenes, but the brand now works with Onofre Ortiz to make their espadín, and with other nearby producers to make limited-edition batches such as the tepeztate from Felipe Cortés.

Pensador are passionate about sustaining the environment where their spirit comes from. To this end, they donate to support water security in the area with the help of Sacred, a non-profit organization founded by *Agave Roadtrip* podcast host Lou Bank to support indigenous communities.

Recently, Ben has developed a new brand of tequila called Desdeya. Both Pensador and Desdeya are B-Corp certified. B-Corp certification is managed by B Labs UK, a non-profit that looks into companies' operations and supply lines, analysing whether they are treating their suppliers, customers and the environment with fairness and compassion.

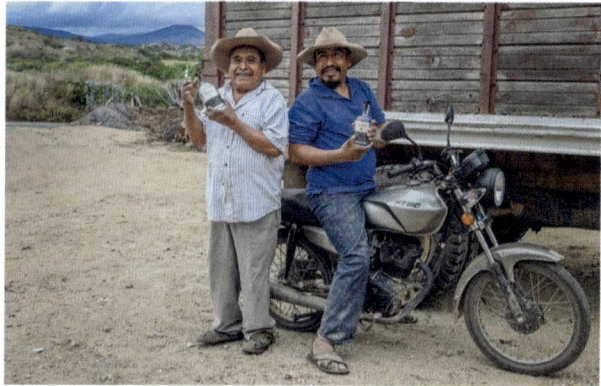

RECOMMENDED PENSADOR MEZCALS

Ensamble	Espadín	Especial, Tepextate De Felipe Y Ageo
48% ABV	47.5% ABV	47% ABV
Notes: leather, sandalwood, fruit, cacao, oak	Notes: buttered corn, chillies, herbs, honey, tobacco smoke	Notes: umami, green pepper, coriander, jalapeño, seaweed

SCORPION

Scorpion is one of those mezcal brands that falls outside the current parameters for artisanal mezcal certification. Founded in 1996 by Douglas French, with the help of third-generation mezcalero Don Lupe – and developed around the same time as Del Maguey – Scorpion was one of the first mezcal brands to reach the US market.

French first came to Oaxaca following his mother, to help her develop a textile initiative hiring local weavers, particularly single mothers. Moving on from that project, he hired the women and, with the help of Lupe, taught them the skill of making mezcal.

Their lack of artisanal status is a challenge. Most consumers who are first learning about mezcal look for this as a stamp of quality, like the terms 'organic' or 'free range'. Scorpion isn't artisanal in the legal sense of the word, but they offer a valuable and tasty contribution to the complex mezcal tapestry.

When I first visited the Scorpion distillery in Oaxaca, I was enamoured with the aesthetic mishmash of old machinery, like

BELOW: *Breaking down cooked agave at the Scorpion distillery in Oaxaca.*

OPPOSITE, TOP RIGHT: *Stainless steel fermentation tanks and copper alembic stills used for making Scorpion mezcal.*

RECOMMENDED SCORPION MEZCALS

Espadín Joven
40% ABV
Notes: herbs, spice, mineral, vegetal

Reposado
40% ABV
Notes: oak, honey, salt, spice,
grassy herbs, lanolin

Espadín Añejo
40% ABV
Notes: smoke, lime, leather,
tobacco, spice

a pleasingly curated junkyard. There's everything from beautiful old vans to milling equipment, interspersed with buckets and plant beds bursting with adolescent agaves. There is a feeling that nothing is wasted; everything is patched and upcycled.

Despite the rustic aesthetic appreciated by most agave aficionados, the use of an autoclave puts Scorpion mezcal outside the parameters for artisanal mezcal. The autoclave is essentially a big pressure cooker. It speeds up the process a little and allows for a slightly larger cook – about 15 tonnes of raw agave – than most artisanal pit ovens. On the transition from wood-fed brick oven to steam, and eventually to autoclave, French explained that the autoclave is more reliable, consistent and, arguably, more environmentally friendly.

French also went on to repurpose machinery from his textile workshop to make agave presses that separate juice from agave fibre after crushing. This further distanced his style from traditional Oaxacan mezcal. He explained that pressing the agave wasn't necessary before the price of the plants began to rise, but now they press the agave four times so that they waste as little as possible.

French understandably has frustrations at the certification restrictions, while huachicoleros adulterate the market with mixed spirit. He explains that it makes selling a competitive mezcal made from 100 per cent agave almost impossible.

Even a surplus of mezcal is repurposed by French. Whether it is classic espadín, tobalá or douglinskii, he has explored the process of ageing in barrel. At the distillery you can try his varieties of aged mezcals. For anyone interested in aged spirits, it is a treasure trove to get lost in.

SALVADORES

In Tlacolula de Matamoros, Oaxaca, is Casa Palacios, home to Salvadores mezcal, where some delicious, carefully crafted mezcal is produced. The brand is produced and owned by Salvador (Sal) Palacios and his family. They decided to name the brand Salvadores from the word 'salvador' (saviour). This is because they are rescuing skills and knowledge that were almost lost to the family.

Sal's great-grandfather, Tomas Hernández, was one of the first to start making mezcal in the town of Tlacolula de Matamoros, just east of Oaxaca city, around 1900. He ran a small palenque in Tlacolula called El Superior, but later gave up their family tradition of making mezcal after an accident in the family. Instead, they used the land for cattle ranching and training horses.

Having grown up in Tlacolula, in 1989 Sal migrated to the US, but in 2005 he returned with his wife Flor to visit the old Palacios ranch. Walking on the same land where he had trained horses in his youth, Sal dreamed of reviving the family's mezcal tradition.

RECOMMENDED SALVADORES MEZCALS

Tobalá Joven	Cirial Joven	Tepeztate Joven
48% ABV	48% ABV	48% ABV
Notes: herbs, citrus, earth, sweet agave, subtle smoke	Notes: sweet vanilla, intense smoke, earth, tobacco, wood, spices	Notes: herbs, floral, citrus, pine, jalapeño, light smoke

Collaborating with his brother and nephews, in March 2012 he began the construction of Casa Palacios. Maestro mezcalero Flavio Pérez Méndez, with over 30 years of experience, was brought in to help.

The clear glass bottle aims to reflect the transparency at the centre of their brand. The label, which is made from agave fibre paper, includes details of location, method, date and batch number, as well as Flavio's signature. The logo was designed by Oaxacan artist ARCH and shows a single agave with its quiote emerging. The branches create the forms of faces, each branch representing the different people involved in mezcal production, beginning with the mezcalero and ultimately reaching the consumer. The numbers 70–400 are nothing to do with Mayahuel's 400 rabbit children; it is the postcode of the palenque in Tlacolula.

The Salvadores expressions include a mix of cultivated and wild agave, with a line-up that includes an espadín at 42% ABV, espadín at 47%, tobalá at 48%, cirial at 48%, tepeztate at 48%, a reposado and an añejo. Recently they have experimented with adding other elements to the distillate, such as flowers, herbs and fruits.

OPPOSITE: *Sal Palacios at the Casa Palacios distillery, where he produces Salvadores mezcal.*

BELOW LEFT: *Lalo and Miguel Palacios, who oversee production of Salvadores mezcal.*

BELOW RIGHT: *Covering the oven at Casa Palacios.*

ILEGAL

The first palenque I ever visited was one called Mal de Amor (lovesickness), on the edge of Santiago Matatlán, the town known as the world capital of mezcal, which is home to the largest percentage of mezcal producers. In 2013, Mal de Amor was just a simple roadside production, distillery in the back, tasting room in the front.

These days, Mal de Amor also makes mezcal for the brand Ilegal. Ilegal began in 2004, when founder John Rexer began 'smuggling' uncertified mezcal from Mexico to his bar Café No Sé in Guatemala. The history is pretty wild, including guns, pornography and Rexer wading through mud disguised as a priest, getting ripped off numerous times trying to shift his bottles. This history, though, is only part of the reason for the name Ilegal. It also refers to the larger issues of immigration and border control. Many of the palenque workers that Rexer met had been undocumented workers in the US.

The brand has come a long way since Rexer's bootlegging days, and has continued to be outspoken about contemporary issues. In particular, their campaign against Donald Trump during his first bid for the US presidency gained attention, with the words 'Donald eres un pendejo' (safe to say, it's an insult) and a picture of Trump on everything from T-shirts to the sides of buildings.

With Oaxacan partners who wanted to scale their production and bring jobs to Santiago Matatlán, Ilegal looked to expand. To grow as a brand, distributing in the US in particular, most producers end up aligning with major spirit companies. In 2015, the conglomerate Bacardi acquired a stake in Ilegal, and it is currently one of the top-selling mezcals in the market. The skinny glass bottle with wax dripping from the cork is now a staple in most bars that stock agave spirits. With a simple presentation of joven, reposado and añejo, Ilegal mezcal is sold in over 40 countries and has won numerous awards for both its quality and brand image.

OPPOSITE, TOP: *Murals at the Mal de Amor distillery in Santiago Matatlán, Oaxaca.*

OPPOSITE, BOTTOM: *Newly constructed pit ovens at Mal de Amor.*

RECOMMENDED ILEGAL MEZCALS

Joven	Reposado	Añejo
40% ABV	40% ABV	40% ABV
Notes: eucalyptus, mineral, green apple, citrus, pepper	Notes: pear, bitter orange, clove, butterscotch, vanilla	Notes: maple, clove, bitter orange, dark chocolate, sweet agave

LOS DANZANTES

Los Danzantes is another influential brand that hails from Santiago Matatlán. It was founded by restaurateur Gustavo Muñoz Castillo in 1997, joined in 2002 by his brother Jaime. Their methods have been inspiring for many artisanal brands hoping to expand and elevate their production. While Los Danzantes stays within the parameters of the artisanal style, the Castillo brothers had a mission to make the process smoother for their workers. They developed a distillery design based around a staggered gravity scheme to make the physical processes less strenuous. In a further measure to increase efficiency, they recycle water through the palenque, cooling it and allowing it to be reused in the process to avoid waste.

The bottle is unusual and easy to reuse. The thick glass with its dimple effect is very tactile, and the flip-top stopper is stylish. Los Danzantes definitely stays on the shelves of mezcal drinkers long after the original liquid is finished.

There are currently seven varieties of mezcal Los Danzantes: espadín, tobalá, sierra negra, arroqueño, reposado, añejo and pechuga. These varieties are available in the Los Danzantes restaurants and at their award-winning bar Selva, which Jaime developed with Alexandra Purcaru.

Although Los Danzantes is distributed to over 25 countries, as with Ilegal, the international selection is mostly limited mezcal made from espadin presented as joven, reposado and añejo. The mezcals are branded as Los Nahuales in the USA because of trademark issues.

The Los Danzantes team are also behind Alipús, a brand that focuses on the production of mezcaleros from different regions. Products using this style of mezcal branding are known as single-village expressions.

RECOMMENDED LOS DANZANTES MEZCALS

Añejo	Espadín	Reposado
46% ABV	47% ABV	43% ABV
Notes: caramel, vanilla, fruit, spice, cedar	Notes: herbs, citrus, light smoke, sweet	Notes: oak, spice, caramel, herbs, smoke, honey

DERRUMBES

Derrumbes was founded by Sergio Mendoza of Don Fulano tequila, and Esteban Morales, who is best known for La Venenosa (see page 156). The Derrumbes brand works with small-batch distillers such as Emilio Vieyra, highlighting the regional style, geography and best-known agave species. Emilio is a sixth-generation producer, and the first to get certified in Michoacán.

As well as Michoacán, Derrumbes' expressions include Durango, Oaxaca, San Luis Potosí, Tamaulipas and Zacatecas. The bottles have a simple chequered design to showcase the pure spirit within, with each state represented by a different colour. To try a flight of Derrumbes mezcals is to take a journey through Mexico.

Their Oaxacan mezcal is a classic espadín, produced in Santiago Matatlán by maestro Javier Mateo. As with the whole range, it is presented at a fairly high 48% ABV. The taste is a well-rounded mezcal, perfect for kicking off a tasting!

Derrumbes Zacatecas is made by the Bañuelos family using 100 per cent blue Weber, the agave known for tequila. Production in this state is typically like tequila in style, but the Bañuelos family produce mezcal in an artisanal style: it is pit-roasted,

OPPOSITE, TOP: *En route to Derrumbes.*

OPPOSITE, BOTTOM: *Maestro Javier Mateo and his team loading agave hearts into the truck.*

RIGHT: *Esteban Morales slicing off agave leaves to prepare the heart for harvest.*

tahona-ground and naturally fermented before copper alembic distillation. With this mezcal we can experience a more traditional expression of tequilana agave.

Tamaulipas is the rarest from the Derrumbes range; it is one of the only brands exporting from this state. The mezcal is sweet, rich and dry, made from an ensemble of three types of agave. As well as a variety of *Agave americana*, they also use two that are found only in the state of Tamaulipas: univitatta and the excellently named funkiana.

One of my favourites in the range is the San Luis Potosí. This is made with wild *A. salmiana*, which grows naturally in the high plateau of San Luis Potosí, and is low on smoke with light floral notes.

Last but not least, the Durango is a fruity, nutty mezcal and a very popular expression from Derrumbes. It is made exclusively of Durango's endemic *A. durangensis*, and distilled in the small mezcal-making community of Nombre de Dios. Despite the size and remote location, the village of Nombre de Dios is at the heart of Durango's mezcal production. In 2024, it was home to Durango's first instalment of the international agave spirit event Mexico in a Bottle. Most brands looking for a Durango mezcal source from producers in Nombre de Dios.

RECOMMENDED DERRUMBES MEZCALS

San Luis Potosí	Durango	Oaxaca
43% ABV	45% ABV	48% ABV
Notes: floral, herbs, sweet, light smoke	Notes: summer fruit, nuts, mineral, light smoke	Notes: light smoke, mineral, fruit

ULTRAMUNDO

As mentioned, most brands looking for a Durango mezcal work with producers in Nombre de Dios. Until recently, this was also true of mezcal brand Ultramundo, founded by Sergio Garnier. Now production has moved to the family ranch, where Sergio also cultivates agave. He explains that if an agave can survive here, perhaps it can teach us things about surviving in other hostile environments.

Lamparillo is a rare type of agave that thrives in harsh conditions where other agaves cannot survive. Although agaves are inherently built for surviving on only a little water, certain species are also cold-tolerant. Lamparillo matures slowly over 15–20 years, and can survive cold winters in the desert of northern Mexico.

Sergio believes in a semi-domestication protocol in order to preserve both the agave and the endemic biodiversity around them. This essentially means helping the agave in the initial phases and then reintroducing them in a friendly way. In the case of Lamparillo, they help them by spacing out the many clones and collecting seeds to germinate at their nursery.

Going forward, Sergio is hoping that mezcal will help him salvage the amazing ranch in Mapimí, Durango. Mapimí is in a region of the desert known as the 'zone of silence', a surreal landscape; it is not surprising that Sergio decided to call his brand Ultramundo – otherworldly.

When Brooks and I visited Ultramundo in 2023, Sergio lent us two all-terrain vehicles (ATVs) so we could explore. Barrelling around the ranch with a bottle of mezcal, the sky felt close to the ground, clouds swirling above like a turbulent ocean. The coral-like cacti, tendrils of ocotillo and bright purple nopales could have been under water. Even the agave seemed strange, with huge, towering quiotes, unexpected in their abundance.

As well as mezcal, the Durango region is also becoming known for sotol production. Indeed, many producers make both.

RECOMMENDED ULTRAMUNDO MEZCAL

Lamparillo
48% ABV
Notes: sweet, citrus, earth, spice, pepper, smoke

BRICENDA

Although I have had fascinating and informative experiences at brand-led distilleries, it is the intimate family-run productions that I love visiting the most. One mezcalero I see almost every week is José Santiago López. His palenque is in the back of Matatlán, past the church and town square, and you can tell he is home when you see his big green truck sitting outside on the street. The gates open onto a beautiful garden where José propagates various species of agave from seed.

Inside the palenque, his sons Óscar and Josué are learning to manage production under the watchful eye of José and wife Bricenda, known as Bris. There are always stacks of adobe bricks made from waste agave fibres, which is a project that Josué is helping to develop. The family are also working with Oaxacan artisans to make agave-fibre paper.

José hopes to build accommodation at the palenque so that agave enthusiasts can stay over and experience the steps of production from start to finish. A bit like my first trip, the idea is to have visitors stay the night, share mezcal, stories and help keep the fires burning.

Producers like José are creative and ambitious. Although he produces for several brands, including Noble Coyote, Cuish and La Medida, José aims to bring his own label, Bricenda, to market. Hopefully producers like José, with generational experience, will continue to rise up in the industry. Their knowledge of the land and traditional mezcal processes will help agave spirits to become be more sustainable. Cheers to that!

OPPOSITE, CLOCKWISE FROM TOP LEFT:
José Santiago López loading the agave oven at his palenque in Santiago Matatlán, Oaxaca.

Checking the perlas using a venencia and painted jícara.

José's wife Bricenda arriving at the agave fields at dawn with breakfast.

RECOMMENDED BRICENDA MEZCALS

Jabalí
50% ABV
Notes: creamy, vegetal, mint

Espadín
50% ABV
Notes: fresh, citrus, caramel

BRAND DIRECTORY

ALIPÚS

$$–$$$$

From Jaime and Gustavo Muñoz, the founders of Los Danzantes (Los Nahuales in the US). Developed in 1999 to celebrate mezcal traditions from different Oaxacan communities. This also allows for a focus on regional terroir, making the brand a favourite for flights of mezcal.

Each bottle is labelled after the village where it was made, such as Santa Ana (angustifolia 42%), which packs a fruity punch, San Andres (angustifolia 47%), which is intensely floral, or San Luís (angustifolia 48%), which has spice and minerality.

AMORES/AMARAS

$$–$$$

Known as Amores in Mexico and Amaras elsewhere. Founded in 2010 by a group of spirits industry folk. They have a variety of agave expressions and mezcals from different states in Mexico, as well as expressions bottled as Amaras Logia and Amaras Green.

AMANTES

$$–$$$

Produced in Tlacolula, Oaxaca. Originally made by Eric Hernández, production is now overseen by Amando Alvarado Álvarez of Ixcateco. Los Amantes Joven is a 40% triple-distilled mezcal made with espadín.

The additional third distillation gives this mezcal a much more blended approach. The notes are subtle with some citrus and cooked agave.

AUGURIO

$$

Made by sisters Araceli and Berenice Rodríguez, who hand-crush with wooden mallets but use copper stills. The mezcals are light in flavour with notes of cooked agave, wood and citrus, and have a light smoky aftertaste.

AUTORA

$$$

This brand focuses on sourcing tiny-batch Oaxacan agave spirits.

Alipús

Mezcalero Rolando Ángeles, who produces for Autora.

BANHEZ

$-$$$

Founded by Francisco Javier Pérez Cruz as a collective of mezcaleros from San Miguel Ejutla, Oaxaca. There are currently almost 50 producers and agave farmers involved in the co-op, mostly from Ejutla. Although many expressions celebrate the work of a single producer, they also offer a blended batch, which is a good-value pour.

CASA CORTÉS

$$$-$$$$

The Cortés family from Oaxaca have been influential on the artisanal agave spirits market. They also have Agave Cortés, Nuestra Soledad and El Joglorio, while Asis Cortés went his own way with Origen Raíz and Dixeebe mezcal brands.

CONVITE

$$

Made by the Hernández family in San Baltazar Guelavía, Oaxaca, where they make artisanal mezcal, as well as managing agave-growing projects. Some may recognize the distillery from Gordon Ramsay's visit to Oaxaca in the television show *Uncharted* (2021). They offer many varieties, all of which can be tried at their tasting room in Oaxaca's history centre. They also have a 38% espadín designed for cocktails, which has light smoke with some minerality and tropical fruit notes.

CORTE VETUSTO

$$-$$$$

Corte Vetusto was founded by David Shepherd and is made by Juan Carlos González Díaz, a fourth-generation mezcalero. His palenque is just outside the Zapotec town of Mitla, Oaxaca. His mezcal is twice-distilled, first with copper stills, then clay. The range includes espadín, tobalá and two ensemble varieties, and he uses a combination of cultivated and wild agave. The espadín is sweet and earthy with some lingering smoke, while the tobalá is floral with hints of minerality.

CUENTACUENTOS

$$

Cuentacuentos means 'storyteller'. Since 2018, founder Read Spear has been curating small-batch traditional mezcals from across the state of Oaxaca. He works with copper and clay pot still producers.

Del Maguey

CUISH

$$$–$$$$

Founded in 2009 by Félix Hernández Monterrosa. Originally a tasting room in Oaxaca, it offers rare regional pours. In recent years they have begun exporting unusual and well-sourced limited-edition batches. The 45% espadín capon from José Santiago López is a favourite, with its rich berry notes and earthy depth.

DANGEROUS DON

$$

Unusually, the flagship bottle for this brand was not a pure espadín. In 2017 Dangerous Don was launched with a signature espadín/coffee expression made by Celso Martínez López in Santiago Matatlán (Celso's own brand is La Jicarita). Dangerous Don is distilled twice, then steeped with coffee beans before being distilled once more. It's a delicious mix of agave notes and rich coffee. Since then, they have released an espadín and a mandarin expression.

DEL MAGUEY

$–$$$$

Founded by artist Ron Cooper in 1995, Cooper's passion and perseverance have been essential to the growth of the artisanal mezcal market. This is many people's first taste of mezcal, especially the Vida, which is a well-known mezcal for cocktails in most bars. The green bottle and bright labels are easily recognizable, and there are limited editions from different towns, which are described as 'single-village distillates'. They have many regular presentations, as well as continuing to grow and explore new areas. The Chichicapa bottle is popular, if not a cult classic, with rich flavours of roasted agave, nuts and pine.

DERRUMBES

$$$

Founded by Esteban Morales and Sergio Mendoza, this was one of the first brands to offer mezcals focused on highlighting different states. Their line-up showcases the agave and techniques from each state, including Michoacán, Durango, Zacatecas, Oaxaca, San Luis Potosí and Tamaulipas.

DON AMADO

$$$

Made by the Arellanes family (which claims 11 generations of mezcal production) in Santa Catarina Minas, using clay pot stills. Various agave expressions distilled at 46% are imported by Jake Lustig and Haas Brothers run with a profit-sharing model. The Largo (karwinskii) is an old favourite of mine, a bit sweet and smoky, with a creamy mouthfeel and slight hint of spice. There is minerality from the pot stills, but not much.

DON MATEO

$$$

Made by the Vieyra family in Michoacán, this is the product of six generations and is currently managed by Emilio Vieyra. It is possibly the most recognized mezcal from Michoacán, and showcases the region. *Agave cupreata* is endemic to the mountains near the distillery, and they distil it at 46%. It has elegant notes of petrichor and cut grass, while on the palate there is roasted tomato and some spice.

EL MERO MERO

$$–$$$$

Founded in 2011 by brand owner Santiago Espinosa de los Monteros, and made in San Dionisio Ocotepec by Justino García Cruz. El Mero Mero loosely translates as 'the main man' or 'the boss'. They currently have three expressions: espadín, tobalá and tepeztate. The 48% espadín is moreish, with caramelized agave on the nose, then smoke and herbaceous flavours, finishing with surprising notes of light cacao.

Derrumbes

ESPINA DORADA

$$$

Made by the Hernández family, each batch is led by a different family member, including mother Soledad, father Plácido and now daughter Jessica. They moved their production from Matatlán to San Francisco Lachigoló nearer Oaxaca city so that Jessica and her siblings could have easier access to education. They have a very unusual espadín made with mandarin, for which the liquid in their fermentation is swapped out for mandarin juice. The result is a bold, bright, citrusy mezcal, that is rich without being too zesty.

GEM AND BOLT

$$

Made by Ignacio Martínez in San Dionisio Ocotepec. The brand is known for its 44% espadín distilled with damiana herb. The taste of smoke and the herb is quite strong, with some notes of acetone.

GEÜ BEEZ

$$

Owned and run by the García Méndez family, headed by Don Crispín in San Dionisio Ocotepec. The name means 'river of wasps', and refers to the site of the original palenque in the town. The family are dedicated to reforesting endemic agave in the region, and they got their product certified for export in 2018. Crispín's sons Daniel and Rigo have also begun developing their own brands. The 50% espadín has bold cooked agave flavours with a touch of salinity and spice.

ILEGAL

$$

Founded by John Rexer in 2006 and currently produced at Mal de Amor in Santiago Matatlán, Oaxaca. This is an approachable mezcal. The 40% is dry with pineapple on the nose, some zest, and chocolatey notes as the taste develops.

IXCATECO

$$$$

Ixcateco is produced in very small batches by the Álvarez family, using rawhide fermentation in the community of Santa María Ixcatlán, Oaxaca. Cooked agaves are milled by hand with wooden mallets before being fermented and then distilled using small clay pots. Their expressions are as rustic as it gets, showing some lactic, leathery and mineral notes.

LA JICARITA

$$$

La Jicarita is the name of the palenque and mezcal produced by mezcalero Celso Martínez López in Santiago Matatlán, Oaxaca. Celso is also known for making Dangerous Don coffee mezcal. The brand La Jicarita was picked up by spirit importers Frijolotes, founded by Young Jung and Fred Baptista. Although Celso produces many varieties of mezcal, Frijolotes began by importing the pechuga, which retailed at a lower price than most pechugas on the market, making it more accessible for cocktails, as well as sipping. This pechuga was made with espadín, using a secret family recipe that includes a variety of seasonal fruits, grains, nuts and local herbs.

LALOCURA

$$$$

Made in Santa Catarina Minas by Eduardo 'Lalo' Javier Ángeles Carreño. Lalo founded the brand in 2014, and has developed a palenque that is a place of pilgrimage for mezcal lovers. He claims that he developed certain practices and terms in the agave spirits world we know today. His mezcals are cult favourites, well-earned praise considering Lalo's commitment to tradition and environmental practices. Most expressions are 48% or higher, and express the rich terroir of Minas.

LA MEDIDA

$$$$

Mezcales La Medida brings together more than 46 Oaxacan producers. The brand is run by Julián Vidal Gómez

Mezcalero Celso Martínez López

Rambhá palenque

Rodríguez, who began working with mezcal over 40 years ago. It offers a selection of mezcals that reflect decades of long-standing relationships in the agave spirits community, among them a 48% jabalí by José Santiago López that is exceptional. Lemongrass, hay, black pepper, grapefruit peel and leather make it an exciting pour.

LOS OCOTALES

$$$

Artisanal mezcal owned by Samuel Santiago Méndez and his family in San Dionisio Ocotepec. They have a range of expressions made by different members of the family. Their 50% tobalá has citrus, floral and herbaceous aromas on the nose. On the palate, it has mineral and honeyed impact, with a sour/acid evolution and herbal and botanical nuances.

LOST EXPLORER

$$$–$$$$

Brought to market by David de Rothschild and Thor Bjorgolfsson and made by the Ramos family in San Pablo Huixtepec, Oaxaca. They have a range of agave expressions, including espadín, tobalá and tepeztate. It's interesting that they also chose to present the less typical salmiana in their flagship range. At 42% this is a dry mezcal, aromatic and vegetal, with some light smoke. The flavour is charred orange, mineral with some grassy notes.

MADRE

$$

Madre mezcal flagship edition is a 45% ensemble of espadín and Agav karwinskii. It presents notes of sage, earth and minerality with a floral finish.

MAGUEY MELATE

$$

Maguey Melate are known for their mezcalero of the month editions and club. Each month is different, and members are encouraged to give open and honest feedback.

MONTE ALBAN

$

An iconic bottle, the one with the worm. They have only the one expression: 40% espadín reposado infused with gusano. The flavours are oak and acetone with some slightly sweet notes of 'worm'.

NETA

$$$$

Neta was founded by Max Rosenstock and Niki Nakazawa, who work with a cooperative of producers from Miahuatlán, in particular Logoche. The terroir leads to rich, complex mezcals, such as the 2020 ensemble from Hermógenes Vásquez. At 47.5%, this mezcal has slight lactic and leathery notes, but finishes clean with a little spice and smoke.

NOBLE COYOTE

$$$–$$$$

Founded as a collaboration with brand owner Bernardo Sada and producer Eleazar Brena. Brena's palenque is in San Luis Amatlán, where he also has extensive agave nurseries. The tobalá, made by Eleazar, showcases red fruits and roasted pineapple with a little lactic note to finish. The brand has outsourced certain agave expressions, such as jabalí, to José Santiago López from Matatlán.

PENSADOR

$$

The flagship expression for Pensador is produced in Miahuatlán by Don Atenógenes García and his son José. It is 70 per cent espadín and 30 per cent karwinskii, and finished at 48%. Like many mezcals from Miahuatlán, this one is very mineral on the nose and palate. There are flavours of fresh green apple and pepper, with some vanilla. The finish has notes of tobacco.

QUIQUIRIQUI

$$

Established in 2011, this brand partners with families who have been producing traditional mezcal in their communities for generations. They have developed a series of agave expressions and an Oaxacan mole-distilled espadín.

Felipe Cortés, who produces for Pensador.

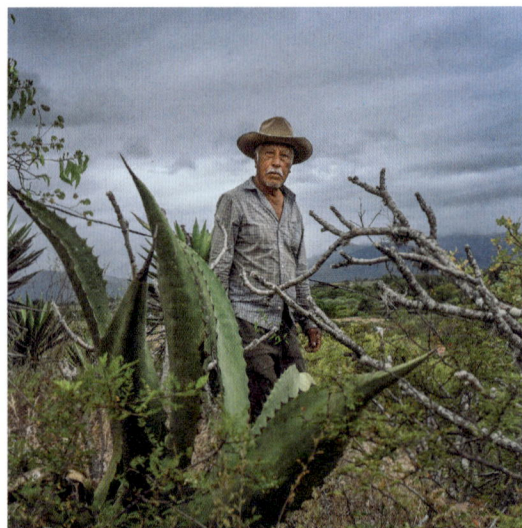

RAMBHÁ

$$$$

Made by Rosario Ángeles Vázquez in Santa Catarina Minas. As a first-generation mezcalera, she is pushing the envelope with this fresh, agave-forward clay pot mezcal. The 50% espadín/tepeztate is funky, earthy and vegetal, with some sweetness of cooked agave.

REAL MINERO

$$$$

Made in Santa Catarina Minas by the Ángeles Carreño family. Originally made by Don Lorenzo, production is now run by his son Edgar, while daughter Graciela manages the brand and has become a legendary speaker on the subject of traditional mezcal. They also launched Proyecto LAM in 2019, through which they research endemic agaves and their pollinators. Their storage room is stacked floor-to-ceiling with amazing mezcals, and you can sample the expressions at their tasting rooms on site and in Mexico City. The karwinskiis alone are well worth a visit, such as the *Agave marteno* expression. Despite being 52%, it is dry with a chalky texture, layers of flavour from dry chillies and pine to baked earth, with sweetness on the finish.

SALVADORES

$$–$$$

Salvadores was brought to market in 2020. It is produced by the Palacios family and maestro mezcalero Flavio Pérez Méndez at the Casa Palacios distillery in Tlacolula de Matamoros, Oaxaca. They have an ever-expanding

Scorpion

range of expressions, including different agave types, barrel-aged examples and pechugas. The espadín comes in 42% and 47%, while silvestres go up in strength. The 47% espadín is fresh with notes of green apple and caramel. It has a great oily mouthfeel.

SCORPION

$$

Founded by Douglas French in 1995, the company uses an autoclave, stainless steel fermentation vats and a mix of copper and stainless steel pot stills. Scorpion is ahead of the curve in ageing mezcal in barrels. The 40% espadín reposado has golden aromas of lanolin and honey. A soft, round entry leads to a dry light-to-medium-body, with honey, grassy herbs, flax, caramel, salt and light spice. It has a dry finish with a honey oak-barrel nose.

Mezcalero Edgar González Ramírez of Tosba

SIETE MISTERIOS

$$–$$$$

Founded in 2010 by the Mestre family, and now in partnership with Chatham Exports. They began working with clay pot distilling producers from Sola de Vega Oaxaca, and they have now included some copper-still expressions. Sola de Vega is known for tobalá, and the Siete Misterios tobalá is finished in clay pots at 50%. It has notes of peach and grass on the nose, and a creamy texture with some ash and caramel on the palate.

SIN GUSANO

$$–$$$

The Sin Gusano Project began as a pop-up mezcal bar in London, founded by enthusiast Jon Darby. The project aims to promote rare agave spirits. Many of these artisanal spirits haven't been experienced outside the communities in which they are made until now. Darby also launched the Mezcal Appreciation

Society (MAS) in spring 2020. This is the UK's sole agave spirits subscription club, which provides members with regular shipments of agave spirits and educational materials.

SON DE LA LUNA

$

In-house brand of palenque Son de la Luna. You can buy numerous expressions under this name if you visit mezcalero Israel Pérez Santiago. Israel is the grandson of Don Tacho, who produces Real Matlatl mezcal. The family is big in mezcal and behind numerous other brands.

TILEÑO

$$

Developed in 2014 by Elias José Ángeles Ojeda to celebrate the history and tradition of the Zapotec people. Tileño is the name of the people from his home town, the Zapotec community of San Martín Tilcajete, Oaxaca.

Elias uses cultivated agave grown around the palenque and makes in the artisanal style. The agaves are cooked in a pit oven, milled by tahona, fermented with naturally occurring yeasts in wooden vats, and double-distilled in copper alembic stills. Tileño has a range of agave expressions that are agave-forward with some light smoke.

TOSBA

$$–$$$$

Developed by cousins Edgar González Ramírez and Edgar González Molina in San Cristóbal Lachirioag, which is deep in the mountains of the Mixe area of Oaxaca. This remote region is rich in flora, including coffee, banana trees, plums and sugar cane. All of these influence the flavours in Tosba mezcal. The espadín is 45%, with layered aromas of spice and pineapple. The palate gets apple and dry cacao.

The cousins have also branched out into an Oaxacan rum called Dakabend.

VIEJO INDECENTE

$$–$$$

Mezcal Viejo Indecente is produced in the small community of San Isidro Guishe, within the district of Miahuatlán in Oaxaca.

Like other Viejo Indecente expressions, the 47% espadín has notes of salinity with hints of smoke and minerality. It is vegetal, with sweet, creamy and caramel notes.

ULTRAMUNDO

$$$

Founded by Sergio Garnier using agave from his family ranch in Mapimí, Durango.

Lamparillo is one of the endemic agaves. On the nose, it gives apricot, banana, green peppers, custard and subtle smoke. The nose translates well to the palate, with sweet fruits, pepper, apple and some spice and smoke.

VAGO

$$–$$$$

Founded by Judah Kuper and Dylan Sloane. While travelling through Mexico, Judah had to go to hospital, and there he met his wife, Valentina. Her father, Aquilino García López, produced mezcal in Candelaria Yegolé, Oaxaca. Together they developed Mezcal Vago. Now Vago works with four small-batch mezcal productions, both artisanal and ancestral. In 2017, Vago began using different-coloured labels for different mezcaleros. Aquilino's family (tan) and Joel Barriga (gold) distil in copper. Emigdio Jarquín (blue) distils in copper with a refrescador, and Salomón Rey Rodriguez or 'Tío Rey' (red) distils in clay pots.

Ultramundo

TEQUILA

TEQUILA TOWN AND REGION

Santiago de Tequila (usually known just as Tequila) is both a town and a municipality in the state of Jalisco, about 60 kilometres (37 miles) from the city of Guadalajara. This bright and vibrant place is a UNESCO world heritage site and one of Mexico's pueblo mágico (towns granted special cultural status by the Mexican government). It is also famously the birthplace of Mexico's best-known drink. The beautiful town is built from the wealth of tequila producers, with large haciendas (ranches) still serving as the major landmarks.

As you get to the central square, there is a bit of a Disneyland vibe. Multicoloured letters declare that you are in Tequila, while shops try to sell you merchandise and terracotta jugs of tequila and juice called cantaritos. Mariachi music clamours outside busy cafés, mingling with the raucous sounds of tourists hopping on buses shaped like barrels or bottles of tequila.

OPPOSITE: *A jimador clearing weeds from around the base of agave, just outside Tequila.*

RIGHT: *One of many vibrant murals in Tequila.*

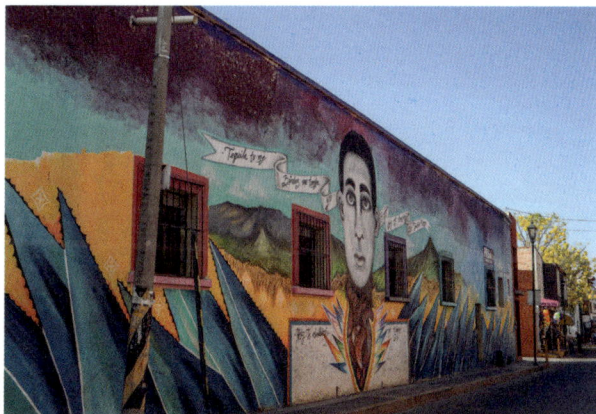

It's hard to think of agave spirits, tequila in particular, and not conjure up the idea of a fiesta, whether it's the iconography that ties these spirits to a vibrant picture of Mexico, or just the buzz they impart. Most of us have raised one too many copitas in celebration. But whether you arrive looking for a fiesta or not, you can't help but embrace the spirit of Tequila town.

The Tequila region lies between the foothills of the Tequila volcano and the valley of the Río Grande de Santiago, which is covered by blue-tinged fields. These slopes of mineral-rich volcanic soil are ideal for growing agave, and many tequila distilleries define their production as high land (los altos) or from the valley (del valle). Aside from altitude, these two regions have different soil compositions and microclimates. These factors lead to different-sized agaves, sugar content and, consequently, flavour profiles.

Highland agaves take longer to mature due to lower temperature and are usually described as being sweeter. Brands such as Tapatio and Patrón come from los altos. Del valle tequilas, such as Fortaleza, are usually earthier with peppery notes.

Brands that make a particular point of using agave from one area should specifically state that they are 100 per cent highland or lowland agave. Some brands will even include information about the particular soil or elevation to help the consumer recognize details of the terroir (for example Tequila Ocho, page 144).

ABOVE: *Stacks of cántaros used for serving cantaritos, a tequila-based cocktail made with grapefruit soda, orange juice, lime juice and tequila.*

OPPOSITE: *Fields of blue Weber agave.*

Pure tequila is made solely from a single subspecies of agave, a variety of *Agave angustifolia* known as tequilana or, more prevalently, blue Weber (see page 29). The plant was given its name by Frederic Weber, a physician and botanist visiting Mexico as part of a French military expedition in the 1860s. Despite the regional name, the DO for tequila allows production in five states: Jalisco, Guanajuato, Michoacán, Nayarit and Tamaulipas. Within the DO, these states can grow the agave, produce, bottle and market tequila. Although some of the additional states do grow agave for the tequila industry, most production takes place in major distilleries (fábricas) in and around the town of Tequila.

HISTORY

When the people of Tequila first started making agave spirits, the product was known as mezcal de Tequila. It was a rustic agave spirit, made similarly to the artisanal mezcals and raicilla that we know today, with a pit oven for roasting the plants, a stone mill for crushing, and small pot stills. They weren't even restricted to the blue Weber agave. Over time, tequila became the most popular agave spirit and became known purely as tequila.

Intimidated by the success of Mexican spirits, which were competing with Spanish brandy and wine, the Spanish King Charles III (1716–88) banned alcohol production, driving many producers into the mountains to conceal their work. Haciendas in Tequila were the first agave spirit producers to receive official permits from Spain, which raised this regional mezcal out of the shady world of clandestine distillation. It is likely that Spain saw the value in taxing this product instead of banning it. The Mexican elite's fondness for luxury imported spirits, including French brandy and Scotch whisky, led the makers of tequila to emulate those other pre-existing spirits.

JOSE CUERVO

The Cuervo family, now famous for the huge brand Jose Cuervo, was one of the earliest to make mezcal de Tequila. Now the brand is part of one of the largest stables of agave spirits, including 1800 and Gran Centenario.

Don José Antonio de Cuervo inherited a production site in 1758, which at the time consisted of some fields and a small distillery producing agave spirits. By 1795, the Cuervo family had been producing tequila for several decades. It was in this year that Don José's son, José María Guadalupe Cuervo, was given the first licence by Spain to produce 'official' tequila.

Cuervo also claimed the first barrel-aged tequila in 1800, which is the reason for the name of their premium aged brand, 1800. As a leader in industry, the brand Jose Cuervo has commissioned artists to help develop the legend of tequila. Early examples show men in charro (embroidered) suits and rosy-cheeked, buxom ladies with bottles of tequila. You can see these in the Cuervo collection and Museum of Tequila.

OPPOSITE: *Tequila town.*

BELOW: *A Jose Cuervo tanker leaving Tequila.*

THE PATH TO INDUSTRIALIZATION

The history of tequila is characterized by boom-and-bust cycles of both agave growth and production of the spirit. Following the Mexican War of Independence (1810–21), there were records of significant growth in the tequila industry. By 1821 Mexico had broken free from Spain. Distilleries surrounded the town of Tequila.

Miners installed in Jalisco were consuming mezcal de Tequila. A trainline connected the mines in Jalisco to Veracruz, and eventually across the border to the US. Along with opals, silver and gold, miners began to load the carriages with barrels of tequila. Demand coming from the mines and further afield led to growth in production.

Mexicans really began identifying with and drinking tequila during and after the Mexican Revolution in 1910, which saw a surge in national pride. Tales of tequila-drinking revolutionaries also crossed the border into the US, fuelling a romantic legend of tequila. The US Prohibition of the 1920s only served to increase appreciation for the drink.

Along with Jose Cuervo, another key brand that shaped the growth of the tequila industry was Sauza. Founder Don Cenobio Sauza originally worked for Jose Cuervo, but in 1873 he purchased his own distillery,

which he called La Perseverancia. He switched from using pit ovens to brick ovens for cooking agave, thus minimizing smoke in production. He was also one of the first distillers to begin exporting his tequila to the US.

At the Chicago World Fair in 1893, Cenobio Sauza's Tequila mezcal won a gold medal, which drew international attention to Mexico's agave spirits. As more people tasted the spirit, there was more demand, which led to further growth. Industrial techniques were reaching Mexico, and the big haciendas began to use these to increase productivity, bringing in stainless steel tanks and industrial technology, replacing more rustic equipment with the aim of making cleaner tequila.

Early campaigns aimed to raise the status of tequila. These included distancing it from mezcal, which was looked down on as a campesino (peasant) drink. After World War II, demand grew in the USA and the Mexican government became increasingly protective of the tequila name. In 1949 Mexico passed laws regulating where and how tequila could be made. Significantly, it was at this point that the standard stated that it had to be made from 100 per cent *Agave tequilana*. The short maturation and high yield made it compatible with the industrial processes that were being adopted.

In 1968, Mexico City hosted the Olympics. Around this time, tequila-based cocktails, such as the Margarita and Tequila Sunrise, became bar staples, before a crash in agave prices in the 1980s led to many distilleries closing their doors. Big brands put pressure on agave farmers to sell at below-market prices. This period also saw agave farmers move into distilling in order to process their own plants. Among them were the

Fonsecas, who had been growing agave since the 1800s. In the 1980s they bought a closed-down production facility, the legendary La Tequileña distillery (NOM 1146) in the heart of Tequila town. Now La Tequileña produces some of the industry's most respected brands, including Don Fulano, Cimarrón, Fuenteseca and expressions for ArteNom.

Production doubled between 1996 and 1999, and tripled by 2008. Financial success in the industry has led to further partnerships, share-holders and international buyouts. Celebrities have also been drawn to the gold ticket of tequila – from actors and musicians to sports stars and Kardashians, there are countless celebrity brands. The most famous of these is probably Casamigos, which was founded in 2013 by George Clooney and Rande Gerber, and acquired in 2017 by Diageo.

The pressures of growth, scale and a shifting bottom line have affected the tequila industry's priorities and business practices, and in particular the production process.

A growing regard for other agave spirits – mezcal in particular – has led consumers to look for artisanal practices behind their tequila, and a premium, 100 per cent agave spirit. They are keen to invest in sustainable and conscientious products that emphasize transparency from field to glass. These trends have led to a fresh aesthetic for new brands such as El Rayo and Los Sundays, and revamped classics, such as Don Fulano.

Celebrities have invested heavily in the tequila industry, inspiring their fans to follow suit. Flavoured tequilas and pre-mixed canned cocktails are also drawing a new audience. From the billion-dollar sale of George Clooney's Casamigos to the success of Kendall Jenner's 818 Tequila, this side of the market is huge, and brings more attention than ever to the category.

There are concerns around whether the capital and selling power of celebrities comes before quality and environmental issues. However, Ivan Saldaña, founder of Casa Lumbre Spirits, who has teamed up with stars including Maluma (Contraluz Cristalino Tequila) and Lewis Hamilton (Almave 0% Alc Tequila), explains that 'it is the personal message they bring that is important. A celebrity who makes environmentally conscious choices will share this through the products they back.'

Rather than getting hung up on the idea of celebrity, we would do better to stop supporting brands owned by multinational corporations. The real names to know are the tequila-makers – among which, Arette, Don Fulano and Fortaleza are great options.

OPPOSITE: *Agave growing outside a production in Arandas, Jalisco.*

RIGHT: *Two different styles of oven used to make Arette at the distillery in Tequila, Jalisco.*

TYPES OF TEQUILA

THERE ARE SIX RECOGNIZED CATEGORIES OF TEQUILA:

BLANCO, also referred to as plata or silver tequila, which is clear and unaged. The purest form of tequila, blancos should feature cooked agave aroma and flavour.

REPOSADO, meaning 'rested', should spend a minimum of two months in oak barrels. A great reposado will complement the taste of the cooked agave, usually adding notes of vanilla and caramel from the toasted interior of the barrel.

AÑEJO, ('aged') from the Spanish word for year (año). The liquid must spend a minimum of a year in oak barrels, and the barrels should be no larger than 600 litres (160 gallons). The result is typically an oaky tequila with a long, complex finish.

EXTRA-AÑEJO (ultra-aged) tequilas spend a minimum of three years in oak barrels. It is debatable whether this is necessary for agave spirits, where the agave sugars can be lost under barrel flavours.

Blanco

Reposado

Añejo

ORO (gold) tequila, sometimes labelled as joven (young). This class of tequila is often a mixture (mixto) made with caramel colouring and additives.

CRISTALINO is a relatively new classification. The liquid is aged like an añejo, but stripped of tannins through processes such as charcoal filtering, so that it resembles a blanco in appearance while retaining the barrel flavour.

All tequila, including 100 per cent agave expressions, are permitted by the NOM to use up to 1 per cent additives, which can be any flavouring agents approved for human consumption by the Mexican government. Additives can include glycerine, caramel colour, sugar syrup or oak extract, and can taste anywhere between vanilla and candy floss (cotton candy). A concern for the agave spirits market is that the consumer palate is manipulated to expect different flavours when they are accustomed to mixtos and additives, rather than the real taste of a pure agave spirit. As challenging as this is, most tequila producers will concede that anything that introduces people to the world of agave is good. That being said, there is hope consumers will move on from the industrial to the artisanal. For more on choosing and buying tequila, see page 183.

Extra-añejo   **Oro/Joven**   **Cristalino**

PRODUCER STORIES

DON FULANO

Since I found myself drinking premium agave spirits, the tequila brand I have had the pleasure of sipping – and visiting – most is Don Fulano, which is produced at La Tequileña distillery in Tequila. The brand was developed in 2002 by Enrique Fonseca and Sergio Mendoza, co-founder of Derrumbes mezcal.

Together, Sergio and Enrique represent many generations in the industry. The Fonsecas come from five generations of agave farmers and distillers. In the late 19th century, they started planting agave to supply the first tequila distilleries, but by the 1980s there was a shortage of the raw material. Many farmers went out of business, but the Fonseca family decided to become distillers. Instead of building a new distillery, they bought the legendary La Tequileña distillery (NOM 1146) in the heart of Tequila town.

Enrique went to Europe to learn about spirits there. In Scotland, he learned about distillation and the different kinds of stills used to create different profiles. He fell in love with the ageing process, the layering of flavours by marrying different batches over time, and the importance of sourcing the right casks. This experience proved invaluable in producing quality aged tequilas at La Tequileña.

Don Fulano is made from estate-grown, mature blue Weber agave. This is cooked in autoclaves before being fermented in volcanic spring water and proprietary yeasts. They blend small amounts of column-distilled spirit (using a copper Coffey-style column still) with a majority of pot-still distillate in order to achieve consistency.

OPPOSITE, CLOCKWISE FROM TOP: *A small gift of unaged Don Fulano going into a barrel for the future.*

Sergio Mendoza with ageing barrels of Don Fulano at La Tequileña distillery.

Inside the La Tequileña distillery in Tequila, Jalisco.

RECOMMENDED DON FULANO TEQUILAS

Blanco	Fuerte	Imperial
40% ABV	50% ABV	40% ABV
Notes: floral, light herbs, tropical fruit, white pepper, mineral, earth, butterscotch	Notes: floral, jasmine, orange blossom, mineral, yellow apple, grass	Notes: fruit, sweet spices, pepper, toffee, chocolate, coffee, tobacco, nuts

FORTALEZA

Aged tequilas used to be the bestsellers, but recent years have seen consumers leaning more towards blanco, or unaged, tequilas. The change means that more people are tasting the truest expression of the agave plant, without the extra flavours that come from time spent ageing in a wooden barrel. Blanco tequilas are excellent for sipping neat or mixing into cocktails. Brooks describes this as a 'mezcalification' of tequila, or a return to artisanal practices in response to the consumer's appreciation for those kinds of agave spirits, and brands such as Fortaleza are among the pioneers of this.

The great-grandson of Cenobio Sauza (see page 132), Guillermo Erickson Sauza, is the founder of Fortaleza. Despite its legacy, Fortaleza is a small, independent distillery that makes tequila traditionally with virtually no modern machinery. They use brick ovens, tahonas, wooden fermentation vats and copper stills. Due to the size of the distillery and style of production, batches are extremely limited in size.

OPPOSITE, LEFT: *Working with the tahona at the Fortaleza distillery.*

OPPOSITE, RIGHT: *Stefano Francavilla discussing different strengths of tequila during the Fortaleza making process.*

BELOW: *Blue Weber agave on the Fortaleza estate in Tequila, Jalisco.*

Fortaleza have thrown open the doors to their production in order to showcase their methods. Bartenders from around the world are invited to visit the distillery, along with the Arette and Don Fulano production facilities. These industry events have created a platform for bartenders to act as natural ambassadors through their enthusiasm about the experience of visiting the tequila production.

In particular, the tahona has become a major selling point for Fortaleza, a shorthand for expressing their small-batch traditional methods. There is much debate as to whether using a tahona makes a perceptible difference to the final flavour, with some people swearing that you can find more complex flavours in a tahona-made tequila. Emma Janzen, author of *Mezcal*, writes that she has noticed a distinct difference between the two methods when compared during brand-concealed tastings, although she wouldn't necessarily qualify one as being better than the other. As she puts it, 'They simply create different flavour profiles.'

RECOMMENDED FORTALEZA TEQUILAS

Blanco (Still Strength)	Reposado	Añejo
46% ABV	40% ABV	40% ABV
Notes: fruit, green olive, butter, earth, black pepper, eucalyptus	Notes: citrus, caramel, sage, vanilla, apple, earth, cinnamon	Notes: caramel, vanilla, citrus, hazelnuts, fruit, nutmeg

EL RAYO

El Rayo tequila was founded by British friends Tom Bishop and Jack Vereker, guided by maestro tequilero Óscar García. Their brand reflects the elegance of modern Mexico, with artwork inspired by the architect Luis Barragán.

Despite its contemporary flair, El Rayo still pays homage to the baseline of tequila: the agave landscape. The label depicts a lightning bolt (rayo) as it strikes a field of blue Weber agave. This references the origin story for agave spirit, in which lightning strikes the agave flower, cooking the heart below (see pages 19–20).

While developing the recipe for El Rayo tequila, Tom and Jack pursued a flavour profile that showcased the agave and would stand up in long serves, such as in a Paloma cocktail. To achieve this, they use 8 kilograms (17 pounds) agave per litre (35 fluid ounces) of tequila, which is slightly higher than industry standard. They also ferment for longer than many other tequilas, which is an important point in the process that develops flavour.

They have focused on a young, creative audience who are not necessarily typical tequila drinkers, pushing the concept of the T&T (tequila and tonic) with a bold, fresh marketing campaign. For a long-time gin fan like me, this exciting agave twist on the G&T is perfect on a beach, at a cocktail party or in a park on a sunny day.

OPPOSITE, TOP: *El Rayo founders Tom Bishop and Jack Vereker learning how to harvest an agave.*

OPPOSITE, BOTTOM: *Inside the El Rayo distillery.*

RECOMMENDED EL RAYO TEQUILAS

Plata	Reposado
ABV 40%	ABV 40%
Notes: citrus, herbs, pepper, spice	Notes: honey, vanilla, gentle spice, fresh herbs, bitter orange

TEQUILA OCHO

Tequila Ocho was created in 2008 as a partnership between Carlos Camarena, a fifth-generation agronomist and third-generation tequilero, and tequila expert Tomas Estes, with the aim of exploring the role of terroir in the flavour profile of tequila. The Camarena family, who also produce for El Tesoro and Tequila Tapatio, have agave ranchos (fields) throughout the highlands of Jalisco, 34 of which are used for Tequila Ocho.

For each expression of Tequila Ocho, they take agave from a single rancho, highlighting the terroir down to the field of agave that their batches are made from. They have also trailblazed in agave research and how to support its pollinators, principally bats.

BELOW LEFT: *Bats are the primary pollinators of agave.*

RECOMMENDED TEQUILA OCHO TEQUILAS

Añejo	Reposado	Plata
ABV 40%	ABV 40%	ABV 40%
Notes: black tea, pepper, tobacco, cacao, coffee, nutmeg, dried fruits, salted caramel	Notes: rich fruits, vanilla, butterscotch, sweet spice, cinnamon	Notes: citrus, white pepper, mineral, fresh cut grass, earth

BRAND DIRECTORY

1800

$$$$

NOM 1122

Part of the Jose Cuervo family and produced at the same facility, 1800 was launched in 1970 as a premium sipping tequila. Despite the premium title and price tag, it is produced using industrial methods. The family produce various special and celebrity-endorsed editions.

ALMAVE

$$

Founded by Ivan Saldaña of Casa Lumbre and F1 racer Lewis Hamilton, this non alcoholic tequila is made by cooking agave followed by a multi-step distillation process done in traditional copper pots, but missing out the fermentation.

There is a blanco and a reposado, the aim of both being to emulate the taste and mouthfeel of tequila for mixing to create no- or low-ABV cocktails.

ARETTE

$$

NOM 1109

The Orendain family named the brand after a one-eyed horse that won for Mexico at the Olympics. It was officially relaunched in 1986 from distillery El Llano. They offer a clásica and artisanal range. The clásica uses an autoclave, while artisanal uses a brick oven. Both ranges include blanco and barrel-aged expressions. The overproof (50.5%) 101 Blanco from the artisanal range is a great sipping tequila. It is herbaceous with some spice and fruity on the nose.

ARTENOM

$$$$

Various NOM-defined distilleries, including 1123, 1146 and 1414. Founded by agave spirits pioneer Jake Lustig. Distillery La Tequileña (1146) produces a premium and delicious extra añejo for ArteNOM 40%. It smells of deep, rich-cooked agave with caramel and earth. The smooth, luxurious mouthfeel continues the cooked agave notes and develops them with caramel, vanilla and oak.

Arette

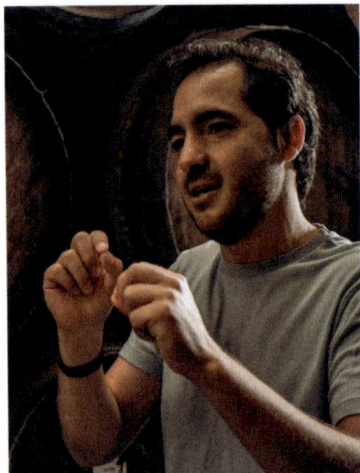
Don Fulano

CABALLITO CERRERO

$$$

NOM 1114 (although not currently listed by regulators), Caballito Cerrero is described as destilado de agave (distilled from agave) instead of tequila. However, it is tequila, since it's made using 100 per cent blue Weber agave and steamed in masonry ovens. Don Alfonso Jiménez Rosales started making the spirit at the Santa Rita factory in Amatitán, Jalisco, in 1968, after separating from tequila Herradura (which he co-founded). His 46% Caballito Azul is one for mezcal fans – it's great as a sipper, being smoky, ashy, musty and rich with agave notes.

CASAMIGOS

$$$

NOM 1609

Owned by Diageo, this is one of the best-known brands of agave spirit due to celebrity founders George Clooney and Rande Gerber. The flavours are sweet, without much agave coming through.

CASCAHUIN

$

NOM 1123

Made at El Arenal in the Los Valles region of Jalisco by the Rosales family since Salvador Rosales Briseño opened the distillery in 1955. It is a traditional, small-batch production using a brick oven and tahona. Delicious and underrated, the 40% blanco is floral on the nose with some citrus, and is refreshing yet earthy on the palate with subtle spice.

CIMARRÓN

$

NOM 1146

Produced by Enrique Fonseca with distillery La Tequileña. It is column-still and pot-still blended for a clean, easy-drinking tequila with notes of green apple and orange zest, with some salt and minerality.

CLASE AZUL

$$$$

NOM 1595

As famous for its ceramic bottle as for its liquid, and definitely a statement item on a bar shelf. Owned and run by founder Arturo Lomeli and co-owner Juan Sánchez, this runs very expensive by the glass, but is better value when bought in bottle. The 40% blanco is smooth, with peach notes on the nose and floral freshness on the palate.

DON FULANO

$$

NOM 1146

Founded by Enrique Fonseca and Sergio Mendoza in 2002 with distillery La Tequileña. They focus on using the best-quality, 100 per cent estate-grown agave, natural spring water and proprietary yeasts. They use pot stills with a little column still blended for consistency, and produce blancos and barrel-aged expressions. The 50% Don Fulano Fuerte is excellent: it is smooth with a clean finish, fruit- and agave-forward and with lasting minerality. This expression won best in show at the San Francisco Spirits awards in 2024.

EL RAYO

$$

NOM 1479

One of the newer brands on the market, with an award-winning bottle design. Made with mature agaves sourced from highland and valley, cooked in an autoclave and distilled with 105-year-old copper pots. Blanco and reposado expressions are available, both at 40%. Light with a smooth mouthfeel, citrus and some agave notes come through with a warming peppery finish. They recommend drinking it like gin, as a tequila and tonic.

FORTALEZA

$$

NOM 1493

Formally launched in 2005 by Guillermo Erickson Sauza and very popular among bartenders. Traditional methods are used, including brick ovens, tahona, wooden fermentation vats and small copper pot stills. The overproof 'still strength' blanco is 46%, and is slightly floral and citrus zest on the nose, with some freshness like eucalyptus. It has full, herbaceous taste, finishng with light minerality.

FUENTESECA

$$$$

NOM 1146

Made by Enrique Fonseca at La Tequileña distillery and exported by Haas brothers. After visiting Scotland, Fonseca laid down barrels of tequila. Some have been ageing since 1998, making them the oldest barrel-aged tequilas on the market. In some instances, these highly aged sips can be more barrel than agave, but they are still delicious, with notes such as sweet spice, tobacco, vanilla and banana.

El Rayo

GRAN CENTENARIO

$

NOM 1122

One of the oldest brands on the market, founded in 1857 by Lázaro Gallardo. These days they use a highly industrialized process. They offer a blanco and añejo both at 40%. The blanco is floral and slightly herbal. The añejo is dominated by wood and caramel.

JOSE CUERVO

$

NOM 1122

The original land for the Jose Cuervo distillery was registered in 1758. There is a huge range of Jose Cuervo on the market. Check out editions such as the Reserva de la Familia, which are more artisanal.

Los Sundays

LOS SUNDAYS

$$

NOM 1438

This NOM is one of the largest tequila-producing distilleries, with well over 100 brands coming out of this single site. Los Sundays is a newcomer, with a focus on flavour-infused tequilas, which include coconut and jalapeño. Highland-sourced agave is cooked in a brick oven, fermented in stainless steel fermentation tanks and then finally distilled in stainless steel pots. The 40% blanco is simple: bright and citrusy. Their marketing suggests that drinking Los Sundays is a lifestyle choice.

PATRÓN

$$$

NOM 1492

One of the most famous premium tequilas available. Although originally made by the distillery Siete Leguas, this venture ended when Patrón production grew beyond the artisanal methods of Siete Leguas. Now Patrón tequilas are produced at a purpose-built site. They have some traditional elements in their process, which are most evident in their ultra-premium Roca expression. At 42%, the Roca blanco is good for sipping, with earthy, sweet notes of agave and fresh-cut grass on the nose. There's creaminess in the taste, with some citrus and minerality. They also have aged and flavoured expressions, such as the Patrón XO Cafe, which is a 35% liqueur.

Jose Cuervo

have a very smooth texture and are always crowd favourites. The blanco floral has some citrus minerality, while the reposado has cinnamon and light caramel, dried stone fruits with a hint of leather and coffee.

TAPATIO

$$

NOM 1139
Produced at La Alteña distillery, founded in 1937 by the Camarena family and run by Carlos Camarena, who is considered one of the best tequila makers there is. He uses only estate-grown agave and has cultivated a strain of yeast on site for decades. The flagship blanco is 40% and rich with layered flavour. On the nose you'll find some pine, berries and vanilla that complement the silky texture of the spirit. It holds the taste of flowers and tropical fruit.

TEQUILA OCHO

$$

NOM 1474
Founded as a partnership between Carlos Camarena and Tomas Estes. It is a terroir-led concept, with each bottle sharing detailed descriptions of where and when the agave was sourced. ABV is 40% across the range, and all aim to respect the raw material: agave. There are reposado expressions as well. The 2021 El Pastizal blanco tastes fruity with a little brine, with a little vanilla and apple on the nose. Once aged, the spirit becomes more peppery, with musk, molasses and some minerality.

SAUZA

$

NOM 1102
Founded in 1873 by Don Cenobio Sauza, this is one of the oldest and bestselling tequilas worldwide. Distilled at La Perseverancia, now owned by Beam Suntory. Industrial processes include diffusers, fermentation in stainless steel and column stills.

SIETE LEGUAS

$$

NOM 1120
Founded by Ignacio González Varga and named after Pancho Villa's horse, Siete Leguas has been family-owned and run at El Centenario since 1952. Their two neighbouring distilleries have slightly different styles of production and the final product is blended to taste, rather than to a formula. Estate-grown highland agave are naturally fermented, with and without fibres, and distilled in copper pots. At 40%, their tequilas

RAICILLA

Raicilla is a small-batch agave spirit made in the state of Jalisco. The culture of raicilla in many ways resembles that of tequila 300 years ago. Today, raicilla and tequila are very different when it comes to production methods, culture and flavour. The key difference is that tequila became an official category in 1974, whereas raicilla did not receive a DO until June 2019. The alcohol in raicilla is derived purely from agave sugars, whereas many tequilas are mixed with cane sugar and other additives. While 100 per cent tequila can only legally be distilled from blue Weber agave, raicilla may contain various types of agave, but not blue.

Commercial raicilla brands have long been subject to the same health and safety regulations that govern all alcoholic beverages for legal sale. But unlike the highly regulated tequila industry, there are still many raicilla producers working without any certification or legal recognition. The majority of raicilla brands are not available outside Jalisco. However, some do make it out of the country and can be found via online distributors, and in a few bars with exceptional agave spirit selections.

The word 'raicilla' comes from the Spanish for 'little root'. One suggestion for this name is that when the Spanish saw the heart of the agave plant they mistook it for a root. However, it is more probable that the name came about to disguise the spirit and dissociate itself from mezcal during times of prohibition. Clandestine producers would claim that their product wasn't the illicit agave spirit but a type of 'root-infused tonic'. I have heard this term continuing to be used to avoid taxation; producers sometimes refer to it as a medicinal drink and not an alcohol.

The producer is known as a raicillero or tabernero. As with other agave spirits, a distinguished producer is often referred to as maestro. They work in tabernas, which are similar to the palenques of Oaxaca.

OPPOSITE: *Don Alberto Hernández with some of his delicious raicilla.*

As with many artisanal agave spirits, people's first taste of raicilla is often described as transformative. Raicilla often surprises mixologists because of its delicate nature; it doesn't overpower cocktails because without strong smoke notes from the cook, floral and botanical characteristics can shine. These flavours are comparable to many gins, so the cocktails you could make with gin can also be made with raicilla. The raicilla adds depth and agave notes, making it a creative addition to any gin cocktail, but it also works in a wide range of drinks.

ABOVE LEFT: *Raicilla dripping out of the still.*

ABOVE RIGHT: *Raicilla in a glass garrafon (water cooler jug).*

OPPOSITE, TOP: *A Filipino still made from the wood of the bonete tree.*

OPPOSITE, BOTTOM: *An adobe oven used for cooking agave to make raicilla.*

THE LANDSCAPE

There are two main regions for raicilla production in Jalisco: coastal (de la costa) and mountain (de la sierra). The two varieties of raicilla do not share a common terroir; the landscapes and climates differ vastly,

which creates fundamentally different flavour profiles. Like all mezcal, the flavour can vary wildly depending on the types of agave used and where it is made. I find that coastal raicilla tends to have more briney qualities, perhaps because agaves from the coast grow in a salty environment. Mountain raicillas, on the other hand, tend to be more floral.

Sierra (mountain) raicilla is produced primarily in and around the municipalities of Mascota and San Sebastián del Oeste, which are cool and covered in pine forest. The coastal style is usually found in the vicinity of Cabo Corrientes, a rural municipality just south of Puerto Vallarta. While Vallarta is known for its beaches and high-rise hotels, Cabo Corrientes is a remote stretch of coast known for its amazing raicilla.

The other major difference between the two regions is the species of agaves. Coastal raicilla is made primarily from *Agave angustifolia* and *A. rhodacantha*, while mountain raicilla is made primarily from *A. maximiliana* and *A. inaequidens*. The agave used is generally semi-wild or cultivated, as truly wild agave is now quite scarce in the raicilla

regions. Semi-wild agaves are planted, but then left to themselves for many years until they reach maturity. The raicilla NOM specifies that mature agave must be used.

As with many artisanal agave spirits, people often describe the first taste of raicilla as transformative. Here are tasting notes of a coastal raicilla made by Jon Darby, founder of Sin Gusano:

> Wow, the first sip is a huge, palate-filling delight. Elote [roasted sweetcorn] with all the butter and cheese, overlaid with tropical fruits. It seems to get thicker in the glass and becomes a wonderful blend of fruity and woody sweetness mixed with strong lactic and cheesy tones.

The Sin Gusano project works with agave spirits from throughout Mexico. Since beginning their project in Oaxaca with small-batch mezcals, they have added raicilla to their stable of artisanal spirits, working with limited-edition batches, exporting raicilla from both regions. Their mountain raicilla is deemed more approachable for those newer to the category.

PRODUCER STORIES

LA VENENOSA

This is one of the most widely distributed raicillas, and is curated by my esteemed friend and road-tripping guide Esteban Morales. La Venenosa offers expressions from many renowned coastal and sierra producers.

The artwork for La Venenosa labels was inspired by petroglyphs (rock carvings). Each has a different colour to reflect how Morales feels during visits with each producer. With La Venenosa, Morales shares a rainbow of raicillas that reflect the diversity of Jalisco.

As well as La Venenosa raicilla and Derrumbes mezcal, Morales has been a trailblazer for the distribution of other Mexican spirits, including bacanora and sotol.

I was lucky to be with Esteban when making my first visit to raicilla producers. We visited some legendary taberneros who produce for the La Venenosa range, including Don Luis Contreras from the Sierra del Tigre and Don Alberto (Don Beto) Hernández. Don Luis (orange label) uses a pit oven to cook wild *Agave inaequidens*, known locally as 'bruto', and distils in clay pots. Don Beto (green label) cooks his agave in an adobe oven and uses Filipino-style stills (see photo page 153).

Esteban founded La Venenosa in 2011, and against the odds has brought both his brand and the broader raicilla category to the international market. In addition to La Venenosa and Mezcal Derrumbes, Esteban's company, Casa Endémica, also distributes La Higuera sotol and YooWe bacanora.

OPPOSITE: *Don Luis Contrera collecting raicilla from his clay pot stills.*

RECOMMENDED LA VENENOSA RAICILLAS

Raicilla Sur
47% ABV
Notes: pepper, sweet leather, mineral, candied fruit, sugar syrup, floral, spice

Raicilla Costa
45.5% ABV
Notes: wood smoke, fruit, sweet spice, herbs, pepper, mint, mineral, aniseed, lemon

Raicilla Sierra
42% ABV
Notes: sweet lemon, apple, butter, mineral, spice

EL VIAJE

In 2019, Andrew Bernauer began developing his project El Viaje Spirits. His flagship product is the El Viaje raicilla, made by raicillero Benito Salcedo Ríos. It is produced on a multi-generational family farm outside the town of Mascota in the sierras of Jalisco.

Bernauer initially envisioned starting a tequila brand, but when he realized how saturated the market was, he pivoted to researching artisanal agave spirits. Deciding between coastal or mountain raicilla expressions, Bernauer explains that he was drawn to the mountain flavours: 'I found the mountain raicillas to have an incredible floral and botanical nose, and flavour notes of citrus that really impressed me.'

Benito's family own the land around the taberna, where he and his staff are constantly planting the agaves to replace the ones they harvest. This, Bernauer explains, means that they are not affecting a wild ecosystem, but rather 'producing the raicilla in a sustainable manner, which is critical for ethical production'.

RECOMMENDED
EL VIAJE RAICILLA

El Viaje
44% ABV
Notes: floral, bright citrus, vanilla, earth, vegetal

LEFT: *Pouring raicilla between two jícaras to check the viscosity of the spirit.*

LA XAMANA

BELOW RIGHT: *Tasting La Xamana raicilla at the palenque. The tasting notes are similar for each expression but with different levels of intensity in flavour depending on the ABV, with flavours that linger more at 55%.*

Claudia López Acevedo founded La Xamana raicilla, made in the sierras. She remembers that the first time she tried raicilla 'it shocked me because I felt its magic, its power'. The label shows the moon, sun, agave and compass. The moon holds the agave, which is protected by the sun, with the arrows projecting to four corners, where there are symbols for earth, air, wind and fire. The 'x' also stands for MeXico and Xamana.

Acevedo explains that together these images celebrate the circle of life on Mother Earth, while elevating the elements used for making raicilla. The style is simple and elegant to reflect the feminine qualities she finds in the spirit. She prefers drinking raicilla straight. However, in the summer, she loves to drink raicilla and tonic, as it's easy and fast. 'I add rosemary so it's super refreshing and simple. You can feel the flavour of the raicilla. Other cocktails I love are Negronis and Carajillos. I don't really like cocktails when they are mixed with fruits because you don't taste the raicilla.'

For coastal raicilla, look for Mezonte made by Hildegardo 'Japo' Joya.

RECOMMENDED LA XAMANA RAICILLAS

Artesanal 55%	Artesanal 44%	Artesanal 40%
55% ABV	44% ABV	40% ABV
Notes: honey, dried fruits, nuts, mint, anise, floral	Notes: honey, dried fruits, nuts, mint, anise, floral	Notes: honey, dried fruits, nuts, mint, anise, floral

BRAND DIRECTORY

BONETE

$$$

Bonete raicilla costa is produced by maestro tabernero Joaquin Solis in the state of Jalisco. It is made with 60 per cent maguey Chico Aguillar (*Agave angustifolia* haw) and 40 per cent maguey Amarillo (*A. rhodacantha*). This raicilla is then distilled twice in wooden stills carved from the oyamel tree. It has leather and citrus on the nose, and is sweet and lactic at first sip, with some smoke at the back.

EL VIAJE

$$

Founded in 2019 by Andrew Bernauer and produced in the mountains of Jalisco by raicillero Benito Salcedo Ríos. Made with *Agave maximiliana* slowly cooked in a traditional adobe oven sealed with mud to retain heat and distilled in stainless steel. It showcases bright citrus, creamy vanilla and a deep earthiness, all underpinned by the bold essence of agave.

ESTANCIA

$$

One of the first raicillas I ever tried, this is made by Rio Chenery in La Estancia de Landeros, about a kilometre (half a mile) above sea level in the hills of Jalisco. He uses *Agave maximiliana* grown on a semi-forested ranch with rich volcanic soils. The agave is roasted in an adobe oven for two days, then fermented in clay pots. Once fermented, it is distilled in copper alembic stills. This is a light raicilla with some pine and salted caramel notes, and minimal smoke to the taste.

LA VENENOSA

$$$

La Venenosa's raicilla range was created by Esteban Morales. Every one of its raicilla expressions is unique, created by different maestro taberneros in distinct regions, from different species of agave and using diverse techniques; the individual results are unique and delicious. The ABV of each La Venenosa may vary slightly by batch. Their expression by Luis Contreras is made in the Sierra del Tigre at about 2,000 metres (6,500 feet) above sea level. It is made from very small batches of *Agave inaequidens* that grows wild in nearby coniferous forests. It is roasted over wood embers in an earth oven. The still used for this raicilla is ceramic, Filipino style. The final flavour is unusual and funky, with notes of blue cheese.

LA XAMANA

$$

Made in San Sebastian Oeste, Jalisco. Agave is cooked in a traditional adobe oven, hand-mashed, naturally fermented and then distilled in stainless steel with a copper coil. Finished at 44%.

LAS PERLAS

$$$

Las Perlas is distilled at Hacienda El Divisadero by fifth-generation raicilleros, the Díaz Rubio and Díaz Ramos families. The taberna is located near the village of Las Guásimas in the Cabo Corrientes municipality. They have an expression made with a wild agave called Chico Aguilar. The first distillation is done in a small stainless steel pot still, then it is distilled for a second time in a wooden Filipino still with a copper top. It is a fresh, citric raicilla with light lactic notes.

RAICILLA DE UNA

$$–$$$

De Una is made from *Agave maximiliana* in the highlands of the Sierra Madre Occidental mountains of Jalisco.

Tres Perros Negros

Roasted in an adobe and stone oven, De Una is double-distilled. On the nose it has notes of grapefruit and petrichor. To taste, there are complex spicy notes of black and green peppercorn mixed with raw cacao, getting sweeter with each sip and revealing hints of roasted pineapple.

SAITÉ

$$

Saité means 'cooked agave' in Huichola (Wixárika), an indigenous language in Jalisco. This raicilla is from Colotitlán, Jalisco, and is made using wild agave. Maestro Edgar Saul Covarrubias uses a masonry oven and mechanical mill, then ferments in stainless steel vats and distils in stainless steel alembic stills. This makes for aromas of wet earth, pepper and cinnamon. The taste is herbaceous, with the caramel of cooked agave coming through.

TRES PERROS NEGROS

$$

The brand slogan is 'Because life is more beautiful next to our best friends', and a percentage of sales goes to help dog shelters. Made from *Agave maximiliana* in the mountains of Jalisco, they use a mix of copper and stainless steel stills. On the nose, the first impression is of grappa. The first sips are light and creamy with hints of vanilla peach yogurt. There is very little smoke to it, but there is minerality. The lactic qualities come through more as you keep drinking, adding some funk to the tasting experience.

BACANORA

Bacanora is a rich and smoky agave spirit with peppery, mineral notes. These flavours are due to the agave plant, along with the soil and climate of Sonora, a mountain desert state in northern Mexico. The result is an agave spirit, technically a mezcal, legally defined as bacanora.

Despite similarities to mezcal, Sonora falls outside the mezcal DO, so bacanora cannot be labelled as mezcal. However, locals may still describe it as mezcal or vino. It is typically handcrafted in small batches in distilleries called vinatas, and has to be twice-distilled from 100 per cent agave. The word 'vinata' is likely to come from 'vino', as in vino de mezcal.

Historically, bacanora was made in the Sonoran desert. However, this desert doesn't stop at the border between Mexico and the US, but continues up into central Arizona. In the early days, spirit production bore no national allegiance, and there are records of bacanora production in Tucson and throughout southern Arizona.

In 2000 bacanora received a Denomination of Origin, which states that it can be made only in a few selected municipalities within Sonora. This is niche compared to the broad reach of the mezcal DO, or even the tequila DO.

As with tequila, bacanora is not only the name of the spirit, but in fact a place itself. It is a small town in the Bacanora municipality to the east of Sonora state, which lies in the foothills of the Sierra Madre Occidental mountain range. Pre-conquest, this territory was occupied by the Opata Joba people, and the name comes from the Opata language: baca, meaning reed, and nora, meaning slope. The region is divided by the Bacanora River, which flows from south to north. The area is biodiverse, with fauna including deer, pumas, coyotes, jaguars, lynxes, owls and eagles. The economy is based largely on raising cattle.

OPPOSITE: *The hands of a bacanorero (producer of bacanora).*

ABOVE: *Mules are used to harvest agave in difficult-to-reach mountain regions.*

ABOVE: *Pouring spirit between two jícaras to check the ABV.*

HISTORY

There are records of bacanora being made and consumed hundreds of years ago. In the 18th century, a German Jesuit missionary called Ignaz Pfefferkorn reported the use of this agave spirit in his journal *Sonora: Description of a Province*. Indeed, he praised the spirit for curing him when he was sick:

> Once, while in Sonora, I had these spirits to thank for the restoration of my health. I had so upset my stomach that during a period of six months I could retain no food and had been completely weakened by frequent and violent vomiting. An honest Spaniard advised me to take a small swallow of mescal spirits every day one hour before the noon and evening meals. I heeded him, and my health was completely restored in a short time.

Although Pfefferkorn specifically mentions Spaniards, other evidence indicates that indigenous people were also distilling in Sonora by the 18th century. Agave has been cultivated in Sonora since at least AD 1000.

Due to a strict alcohol prohibition in Sonora during the 20th century, which lasted 77 years, portable stills are common. It is also the likely reason for the diversity and improvisation of tools used to make bacanora: equipment was used that could be explained away as being for another usage if the production was raided.

Although there were restrictions on alcohol production throughout Mexico, governor Plutarco Elías Calles of Sonora was particularly against it. Perhaps this is because his father was supposedly an alcoholic, or it could have been a reaction to major growth in the industry around 1900. During a ten-year period (1900–10), bacanora production doubled. In 1900 there are records of 70 distilleries operating throughout the state that produced 436,406 litres (115,000 gallons) a year, but by 1910 they were producing 832,111 litres (219,000 gallons) a year. Most of this production was consumed within the state, but it was also sold in the states of Sinaloa, Baja California and Arizona. Although bacanora production provided many jobs, Calles saw alcohol as being responsible for decadence and moral perversion. He blamed alcohol for the failing economy and perceived it to be a moral issue.

Calles enforced a ley seca (dry law) in 1915. This was very strict, and producers could be punished by death if caught making spirits. This law was extremely unpopular and in 1919 it was revoked for most types of alcohol, such as wine and beer. However, bacanora remained illegal, and producers continued to be targeted by the authorities.

Hiding from the authorities led to bacanora being produced in smaller bottles that were hidden in walls and false floors; the drink became known as the 'secret of Sonora'. It was only the international success of tequila and mezcal that eventually led to the legalizing of agave spirits in Sonora.

The DO was announced in November 2000, which now protects 35 municipalities in the Sonoran mountains to make mezcal under the name bacanora. These 35 municipalities around the town of Bacanora all share NOM 168.

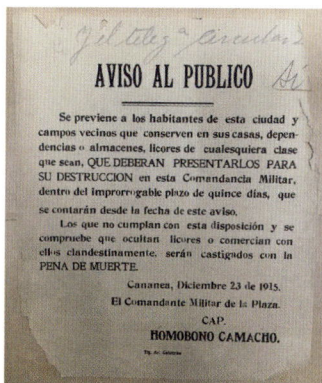

AVISO AL PUBLICO

Se previene a los habitantes de esta ciudad y campos vecinos que conserven en sus casas, dependencias o almacenes, licores de cualesquiera clase que sean, QUE DEBERAN PRESENTARLOS PARA SU DESTRUCCION en esta Comandancia Militar, dentro del improrrogable plazo de quince días, que se contarán desde la fecha de este aviso.

Los que no cumplan con esta disposición y se compruebe que ocultan licores o comercian con ellos clandestinamente, serán castigados con la PENA DE MUERTE.

Cananea, Diciembre 23 de 1915.
El Comandante Militar de la Plaza.
CAP.
HOMOBONO CAMACHO.

ABOVE: *A Public Notice warning bacanora producers to destroy their product. Translation (second paragraph): 'Those who do not comply with this provision and are found to be hiding liquor or dealing with it clandestinely, will be punished with the PENALTY OF DEATH.'*

MAKING AND DRINKING

Bacanora is made from the *Agave angustifolia* haw, also known as the pacifica or yaquiana agave, which matures at around eight years old. The plant grows both in the wild and on farms. While it is very similar to espadín from Oaxaca, it has adapted to survive the Sonoran landscape.

Although the DO specifies the region in which bacanora is made, and is strict on raw materials, it is quite loose on production methods.

As in most artisanal and ancestral production, the process of making bacanora begins with harvesting mature agave, which is then piled into a pit to cook. Additional smoke is imparted and producers often use mesquite as the wood of choice. The pits are commonly sealed with a metal lid and earth, and the agave is left to cook over embers for two to four days.

At bacanora Santo Cuviso they use a conical oven that can process 2.5 tonnes of agave at a time. This is about a quarter of a typical artisanal oven in Oaxaca. Volcanic stone and nopales are used to moderate the flame, and everything is covered with earth and palm leaves.

Once the agave is cooked, it would traditionally be broken down with axes, or beaten with wooden mallets in a canoa. Recently, mechanical shredders have also been introduced to the making of bacanora. The mash can be fermented in the producer's vessel of choice, which includes steel oil drums, large plastic tanks typically used for storing water, or underground reservoirs known as barrancos.

Stills too are often made from steel drums and repurposed water heaters augmented with copper pipes. Although bacanora is typically twice-distilled, a tren may also be used. This is similar to Oaxaca's refrescadera. Made up of two oil drums, one drum acts as the pot and the other as the condenser.

Typically, most bacanora is clear, pure agave spirit. However, there are also two local infusions made with uvalama and anise. Uvalama is a small fruit a bit like a black grape, which grows in the mountains of Sonora. When infused in the spirit, it adds some colour from tannins in the skin of the fruit, as well as a subtle sweetness.

The limited production region and subsequent terroir, as well as the use of specific types of agave, makes bacanora a more clearly defined

ABOVE: *A traditional pit oven.*

DO than that of mezcal, and minimal industrialization in the process distances it from tequila.

The growing popularity of bacanora enriches the range of agave spirits. Choosing to drink bacanora helps the category gain momentum and benefits the wider world of agave. Sharing spirits from different areas helps to take pressure off popular regions, reducing exploitation of single agave types.

The cowboys of Sonora have been known to drink their bacanora from a glass flask called a pachita to stay warm while herding cattle in the mountains. However, the main way of drinking it is usually sipped neat from a caballito (small glass).

Bacanora-maker Roberto Contreras explains that locals 'mostly drink bacanora straight. But a cup of bacanora with a side of cold beer is used as well. We call those paridas.' Another tradition of the people from the Sierra is to drink a shot of bacanora early in the mornings on an empty stomach. They call this 'hacer la mañana' (make the morning).

As bacanora was banned for so long, there are still just a few brands producing the spirit. A small group of dedicated producers kept the tradition alive during prohibition by continuing to plant agave and passing clandestine knowledge on to the next generation.

PRODUCER STORY

RANCHO TEPÚA

The Contreras family have been making Rancho Tepúa bacanora for five generations on their ranch in the foothills of Sonora. Roberto Contreras currently holds the reins, and decided to follow in his father's footsteps 'because of the love I have for the ranch. There's an unexplainable satisfaction that the work I get to do every day brings to me. Waking up early in the morning, surrounded by vegetation, cattle, horses, and other wild animals.'

Rancho Tepúa is located in between two creeks, one on the north side, the other on the south. Water scarcity during drought season becomes a problem in the region, but there are seven different natural water springs, and this is the water Contreras uses for fermentation. He found six old vinatas near some of these springs, which at one point were used for mezcal production. The older ones used the barranco fermentation method.

Contreras has been working with the Institute for Research in Food and Development in Hermosillo, the capital of Sonora. Together they have been experimenting with different strains of yeast to better understand the way they influence flavour. They have also been investigating the nuances of variants within the *Agave angustifolia* haw species used in bacanora. To reduce the pressure on wild agave, Contreras has begun a programme of planting agaves he will need for the future. He has over 150,000 plants that he began in a nursery, and has since transplanted to the hills around Rancho Tepúa.

Producers consider the ideal conditions for *A. angustifolia* haw to be where the palo blanco tree (*Acacia willardiana*) is found growing. Fortunately for Contreras, this tree is found in abundance throughout his ranch. He described how bacanora has been commonly used as a precious gift. 'My grandpa was big on giving his bacanora to people he appreciated, or if you visited his house he'd receive you with a cup of bacanora. We do the same at the ranch, with our neighbours and friends.'

RECOMMENDED RANCHO TEPÚA BACANORA

Blanco
44.5%. ABV
Notes: fresh agave, citrus, grass, hint of spice, mineral, peach

KILINGA

$$

Kilinga bacanora silvestre is made in Álamos, Sonora, by maestro bacanorero Rodrigo Bojórquez Bours. Made with mature *Agave angustifolia* haw, it holds smoky caramel notes of cooked agave. There are some floral notes at the finish.

MAZOT

$$$

Mazot bacanora is one of the few female-owned bacanora brands. Emelia Ezrre Becerra runs the business, while her husband Manuel Sr propagates the agave, and their son Sinohe manages the harvest and the vinata – it's truly a family collaboration.

In addition to a classic bacanora, they also have an uvalama-infused bacanora. The uvalama is a grape-like fruit that grows locally. The infusion is very novel and also tastes like fruity grapes.

PUNTAGAVE

$$$

With over 25 years of experience in the agave distillate industry as an importer and brand owner, Juan Pablo Garciabueno of Tequila Specialists launched Puntagave to express the distilled flavours of Mexico. Each bottle has depth of flavour and character, but is still very approachable for those who are just venturing outside the world of tequila. Puntagave is made

by two different producers: Roberto Contreras of Rancho Tepúa and Jorge Rivas. The mouthfeel is thin, with a lot of fruit and funkiness in the flavour.

RANCHO TEPÚA

$$

Owned and produced by maestro bacanorero Roberto Contreras, a fifth-generation producer from Sonora. Cooked underground for 36 hours and then fermented with wild yeasts in stainless steel vats for 8–10 days. It is then distilled twice in an alembic still that has a stainless steel pot and a copper condenser. The ABV changes slightly from batch to batch. Dry, mineral and citric on the nose, the taste is grappa-like, with light creaminess like peach yoghurt and little smoke.

SANTO CUVISO

$$

Made by the Chacón family in Sonora. Agaves are roasted over mesquite and oak in a volcanic stone pit for several days, then milled by hand and with a shredder. The juices are then poured into vats to ferment for over a week. Finally, the agave juice is double-distilled in handcrafted copper pot stills. It is earthy with subtle tones of pepper, mesquite and smoked oak.

SOTOL

The word 'sotol' comes from the Nahuatl word 'tzotolin'. meaning palm or sweet head. In the north of Mexico, the term is used for both the plant and the spirit. In some areas, where they use the word 'churique' for agave, it is also called sereque (the Rarámuri name for the sotol plant).

Following in the footsteps of artisanal mezcal and raicilla, sotol is now gaining international recognition as one of Mexico's unique spirits of origin. Its handcrafted quality, organic character and distinctive flavour profile have attracted consumers looking for a unique alternative to the more familiar agave spirits. The primary differences between sotol and other agave spirits are terroir and the key fact that it is not actually made from agave! Sotol is made from the dasylirion, a wild desert succulent plant that is palm-like in appearance.

As a spirit, sotol is thought to have appeared soon after the Spanish arrived in Mexico, and has had an outlaw reputation ever since, partly because it's grown in the border zone, partly because Mexican laws have kept it in an illegal or semi-illegal state, and perhaps in part because people like the clandestine story.

Sotol often gets confused with mezcal because both are recent to the international spirit market; both are high-proof Mexican spirits that are traditionally drunk in small sips, typically accompanied by something sweet or salty. Sotol is usually described as more intense in flavour than most tequila, yet smoother than typical mezcals. It often has bright vegetal flavours with lingering minerality.

The spirit sotol is native to northern Mexico, as well as to southern Texas and Arizona. In Mexico, sotol received an official Denomination of Origin in 2002 and became regulated by the Consejo Certificador del Sotol in 2019. Some distillers in the US are also making spirits

OPPOSITE: *A flowering dasylirion at the Pelaya ranch in Mapimí, Durango.*

that they call sotol, which they can do because the US has not formally recognized the sotol DO.

The majority of sotol produced in Mexico comes from Chihuahua. Durango and Coahuila also contribute, but make up a much smaller percentage. The DO has legal status in Mexico, but only limited effect outside. Typically, sotols are divided into two main regions, desert and forest. As with agave, microclimates and soil variations influence the flavour of the final spirit. Different regions and subsequent flavours change how the sotol is drunk. Sotol made in the mountain forest is often paired with something sweet, such as apple slices, while the varieties from the desert are served with carne seca, a dried meat a bit like jerky.

DASYLIRION

The plant genus *Dasylirion* comes from the Greek dasy (thick) and lirion (white lily). This alludes to the plant's arrangement of white flowers. In fact, it is the male plants that have white flowers, whereas female plants have pinkish flowers. There are more than 17 species of dasylirion, each contributing to sotol's rich complexity. The most common varieties are *Dasylirion cedrosanum* and *Dasylirion wheeleri*.

The dasylirion plant is an evergreen perennial that flowers once every few years, unlike agave, which flowers only once, at the end of its life. Dasylirions are thought to be able to live for much longer than most agave. Some producers have told me they think plants could be almost 100 years old. You can tell the age of a dasylirion by the size and the bands on the trunk formed by its multiple flowerings.

Unlike agave plants, dasylirions do not produce clones. Instead, they are reliant on the wind and insects to pollinate them. Aside from having a long time to wait, sotoleros (sotol makers) also have to contend with animals that will eat the plant while it's growing. The plant endures extreme conditions, such as intense heat, cold nights and scarce water. This resilience translates into a flavour that is earthy, herbal and slightly smoky, with distinctive notes of desert flora. Mineral-rich soils impart a subtle but noticeable mineral nuance to sotol, resulting in a spirit that is bold, complex and inherently connected to the land of its origin.

It is believed that sotol has been used in religious ceremonies and as a medicinal remedy for more than 800 years. Like agave, it is also used for its fibres. Indigenous people, such as the Anasazi (Pueblo and Hopi people) and Rarámuri, have been the guardians of this ancestral knowledge. Even now it is common to see decorations for weddings and church adornment made from the inner leaves of the plants.

As with all agave spirits, sotol offers a wealth of variety and flavour thanks to the diverse terroir and different species of dasylirion plants. Most connoisseurs suggest drinking it neat to really savour the nuances of this desert spirit.

In my experience, herbaceous notes and minerality are the defining flavours. However, there are some great sotols with warm, spicy notes. These tend towards cinnamon, sometimes light on the palate, but on occasion gaining the intensity of Big Red cinnamon gum.

There are many bartenders keen to explore sotol in cocktails. As with mezcal and tequila, the complexities of the raw material, along with the personal style of each producer, make this a dynamic spirit to work with.

BELOW LEFT: *A traditional cow horn used for sotol.*

BELOW RIGHT: *A wreath made from dasylirion, representing a crown, on the wall of a palenque in San Isidro Guishe, Oaxaca.*

PRODUCER STORIES

SWEET TEMPTATION

My first experience of witnessing sotol production was when I visited the town of Nombre de Dios in Durango. Brooks and I were halfway through a road trip from California to Oaxaca, and this was our first night back in mainland Mexico. We had an introduction from Sergio Garnier, founder of Ultramundo, to visit producer Juan Manuel Pérez Vázquez of Sweet Temptation vinata.

Our plan was to document Juan loading an oven at his vinata. At 4am we met him at a gas station on the outskirts of the town. The sky was still pitch-black as we followed his truck off the tarmac road and onto a muddy track, which only got muddier as rain began to pour. Bleary-eyed after many long days of driving and the ferry, it was a relief when we turned a bend to see lights from the vinata glowing through smoke and steam coming off the oven.

For over 20 years, Juan and his brother have been making mezcal and sotol for various brands (such as Ultramundo) at Sweet Temptation – the temptation presumably being the delicious spirits they distill. While we were there, he and his team loaded an oven with agave and some sotol; making an ensemble of the two is common. Some of the process was similar to mezcal production I had seen in other states, but with some variations. After cooking, the plants are broken up. Rather than using a tahona, Juan still does it manually with an axe.

The pulp is then fermented for around a week before distillation. The fermentation vats are called tumbas because of their tomb-like shape in the ground. The stills are similar to Filipino stills used in Michoacán – Juan explained that these sculptural stills are known as viejitos (old men).

Producers used to distil on site where the plant grew. They would roast the plant there, then dig fermentation pits. However, with growing interest in sotol, some producers are taking on the industrial methods developed in tequila. Sweet Temptation falls somewhere in the middle, similar in scale to most of the family-run palenques I have visited in Oaxaca.

SOTOLEROS BIENVENIDO FERNÁNDEZ

Bienvenido Fernández was born in 1952 in Madera, Chihuahua, and began making mezcal at a very young age. At that time, his family had to operate in secret, but in 1998 they finally managed to obtain a permit to legally produce sotol. This achievement was not only personal, but also a historic step for sotoleros in the region. To celebrate this milestone, Bienvenido organized a parade he dubbed the sotol burrito. During the parade, they toured the streets of Madera with a cart pulled by a donkey and carrying a barrel of sotol, while a band played *Viva Chihuahua*.

Bienvenido's daughter, Norma Fernández, now represents a fifth generation in the family's sotol lineage. She describes their product as offering intense herbaceous notes with hints of fresh herbs on the nose, as well as nuances of pine, damp earth and light mineral touches. On the palate there is a more earthy and less sweet character than tequila or mezcal. Citrus and spice, such as black pepper or cloves, add complexity and depth to the profile.

This sotolero family also produce for the exciting new brand Parejo. In 2022 Parejo began to buy batches from the Fernández family, with editions made by Bienvenido and his son Juan. Parejo translates literally to 'equal' and is used by vinateros to describe a perfectly balanced sotol. Before they even taste it, vinateros can anticipate the perfect point by assessing the bubbles (perlas) as also happens with artisanal mezcal production (see page 58). However, in sotol, this is typically done by pouring the liquid between two cow horns and seeing how the bubbles dissipate.

BELOW LEFT: *Pouring the spirit from a traditional cow horn into a glass during a tasting.*

**RECOMMENDED
BIENVENIDO
FERNÁNDEZ SOTOL**

Parejo – Bienvenido Fernández
49.4% ABV
Notes: herbs, pine, wet earth, mineral, citrus, spice

HACIENDA DE CHIHUAHUA

This progressive brand, founded over 30 years ago by
Federico Elías Madero, has been leading the way towards
an international appreciation of sotol. It uses traditional
methods combined with more contemporary innovations,
such as the introduction of slow, indirect steam cooking in
mampostería (masonry ovens), the use of champagne and
wine yeasts for fermentation, and ageing in French oak barrels
for their aged spirits.

Hacienda de Chihuahua's unaged sotol has a classic profile,
with fresh herbal aromas – rosemary, mint and sage – followed
by minerality. As it develops, the spirit reveals subtle hints of
citrus and pepper, depending on the product, and finishes with
a slight sweetness on the palate.

RECOMMENDED HACIENDA DE CHIHUAHUA SOTOLS

Plata
38% ABV
Notes: mint, herbs, vegetal, pepper,
mineral, sweet

Rústico
45% ABV
Notes: freshness, herbs, earth

Reposado
38% ABV
Notes: floral, spice, vanilla, oak,
mild herbs, light pepper

SOTOL

BRAND DIRECTORY

CLANDE SOTOL

$$$

This brand presents sotol from different regions, showcasing the influence of terroir on the spirit. The labels on the bottles are colour-coded to represent each producer. The yellow expression is made by Bienvenido Fernández, who cooks the plants in a pit oven for three days, then uses a mechanical grinder before letting the mash ferment with natural airborne yeast in stainless steel tanks. He uses well water to get the desired ABV. His batches are small, ranging from 120–160 litres (450–605 gallons). The expression produced for Clande at 48.6% ABV has notes of banana, wood, cotija cheese, honey and nuts.

DESERT DOOR

$$

This sotol is made in Driftwood, Texas, from plants harvested in the Chihuahuan Desert of western Texas. The variety used is *Dasylirion texanum*. It has thinner leaves than *D. wheeleri*, which is commonly found in Mexican sotol. The plants are cooked in a large steam oven, similar to a pressure cooker. Once cooked, they are machine-shredded and then fermented in stainless steel tanks using proprietary yeast. Desert Door has a custom-made still. The spirit is adjusted to 40% ABV using purified water before being bottled. The spirit is creamy with hints of vanilla and vegetal notes. They also offer a barrel-aged expression.

FLOR DEL DESIERTO

$$–$$$

This sotol from Chihuahua was launched in 2011 by a group of friends after one of them, Flor, won a baking competition using sotol as an ingredient. The plants are wild-harvested in the desert and mountains of Madera. The Cascabel expression is made with *Dasylilrion leiophyllum* at 48% ABV by Gerardo Ruelas, and finished in oak barrels. It is a sotol-based rattlesnake pechuga, incorporating rattlesnake meat during the final distillation. It has a bit of an oily mouthfeel, some anise on the nose, and is fruity on the palate. No obvious taste of snake.

Hacienda de Chihuahua

Hacienda de Chihuahua

HACIENDA DE CHIHUAHUA

$$

Hacienda de Chihuahua is a well-established brand of sotol in blanco and aged expressions. It is operated by Vinomex, and the distillery is located in Delicias, Chihuahua, Mexico. The distillery originally produced brandy. Now master distiller José Daumas Gil de Partearroyo oversees the production, cooking the plants in steam-heated ovens, then ferments with champagne yeast before triple-distilling in a double-column copper still finished at 38%. Their añejo is rested in a new French white oak barrel for two years. Aromas of vanilla, oak wood, floral, light mesquite smoke and light banana. Flavours of spiced orange, mandarin, floral honey, vanilla.

LA HIGUERA

$$–$$$$

The brand's wheeleri expression is produced in Aldama, Chihuahua, by Gerardo Ruelas. The plants are cooked in a pit oven and then milled by hand with axes. Wild fermentation takes place in 1,000-litre (265-gallon) pine vats before being twice-distilled in copper stills. This is a well-balanced sotol with herbaceous notes and some smoke, pineapple and faint nuttiness.

NOCHELUNA

$$

A collaboration between Maestro vinatero Don Lalo Arrieta and Ricardo Pico, master distiller Iván Saldaña Oyarzábal and musician Lenny Kravitz, with backing from Pernod Ricard. The brand has been cultivating dasylirion populations, and claims that more than 850,000 plants were planted in 2022. To make Nocheluna, the mature plants are cooked in an underground pit lined with river stones. The cooked plants are crushed using a mechanical shredder and naturally fermented for 5–10 days. Finally, they are double-distilled in copper pots. The label claims notes of wild herbs, dried stone fruits, caramel and honey, deep minerality and oak firewood.

ORIGEN RAÍZ

$$–$$$$

Origen Raíz is a partnership between the Saravia family of Durango and the Cortés family from Oaxaca. The families were brought together by their sons Asis Cortés and Bildo Saravia. Asis is well known for some of his other projects, such as mezcal Dixeebe. Origen Raíz Sotol is made with wild *Dasylirion cedrosanum* in the mountains of Durango. It has aromas of freshly cut grass, plum grappa and menthol, and the palate is very grassy with some burnt notes.

PAREJO

$$$$

Founded by Jorge Caldera in 2019, Parejo has several expressions from a few different producers. One of the main producers they work with is fourth-generation maestro vinatero Bienvenido Fernández from Madera, Chihuahua. He produces a 100 per cent wild *Dasylirion wheeleri* for Parejo, with an alcohol percentage than can vary from batch to batch. The nose and flavour have hints of spearmint and eucalyptus.

ENJOYING AGAVE SPIRITS

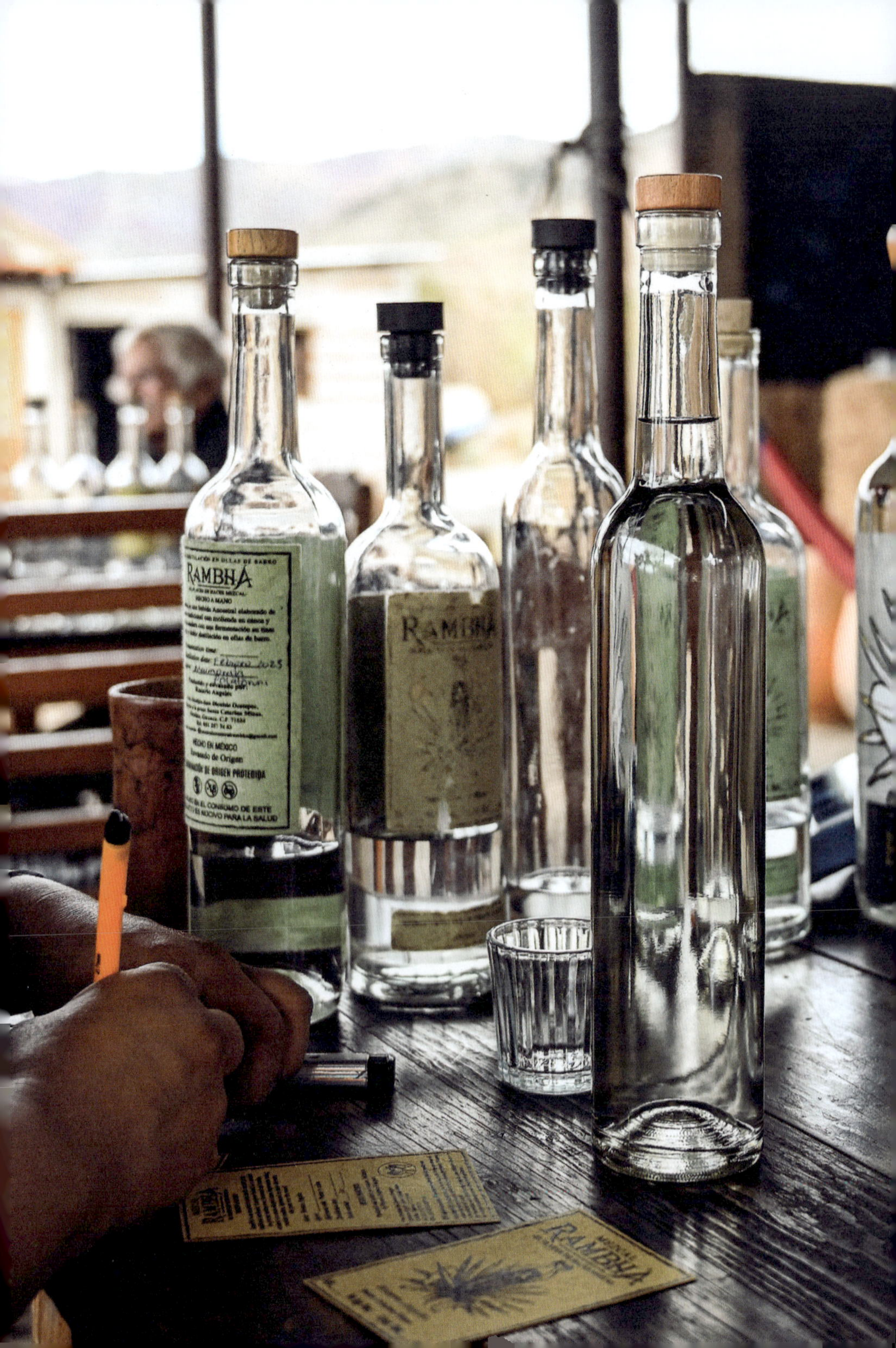
RAMBHÁ
HECHO A MANO
HECHO EN MÉXICO
RAMBHA
RAMBHA

CHOOSING YOUR AGAVE SPIRIT

THE BOTTLE

There is a lot to be said for a beautiful bottle and considered design when it comes to agave spirits. A good label or logo opens the door to a brand's story, alluding to the quality of its product and the long history and tradition that led to this individual bottle.

Bottle shape and weight can help give you a sense of its purpose, perhaps as part of a cocktail or to be displayed behind a bar. Price can also help you to make a choice. However, not all agave spirits are created equal, and not all brands are completely transparent about this. Some brands aim to keep it simple and show off the spirit, while others conceal a lower quality liquid with indulgent packaging.

Back in the day, owning visually appealing liquor bottles was a status symbol, a sign of wealth and sophistication. Now having interesting, well-designed bottles can give 'cool cred' and be a talking point for both those getting into agave spirits and for well-seasoned connoisseurs.

Art and agave spirits have long had a close relationship. From paintings of agave in ancient temples to cutting-edge designs for marketing tequila and mezcal, the drinks and plants have inspired creativity for centuries. Brands can draw on a deep pool of creativity for inspiration: the rituals, traditions, colours and even music of Mexico.

OPPOSITE: *Mezcalera Rosario Ángeles Vásquez signing bottles of Rambhá.*

As explored in the history of Jose Cuervo (see page 131), collaboration with visual artists has been an ongoing theme. Uriel Fernando Barragán Cruz, better known as Bouler, is an artist from Oaxaca. Apart from illustrating the cover for this book, Bouler has produced designs for mezcal, sotol, bacanora and tequila brands. His woodcut engravings are loaded with Mexican symbolism, inspired by his Zapotec roots, as well as the handcrafted processes behind agave spirits. He is also moved by 'the history, legends, and mysticism behind the maguey drink'. He goes on to explain that 'even as mezcal becomes more popular, brands and consumers want to return to the artisanal, handmade, from the design of the bottle [to the] logo and label. Even if there are global design trends, the mezcal industry is very much in favour of the idea that the design of the logo or illustration is also artisanal.'

Trends in agave spirits stem from a need for extensive information on the bottle. Gemma Terry, head bartender at award-winning UK bar Ojo Rojo, explains that their bestselling agave spirits are the ones 'where the details of who, how and where it's made are the clearest. And any that have a great story make it easy for us to sell too.'

There is also an emphasis on purity when it comes to the liquid, which can be highlighted with a simple label. A great example of this is mezcal Pensador, with its black-and-white design and single drop cut-out (see page 101) that reveals the liquid within. At the other end of the spectrum are brands that highlight the vibrancy of Mexican art and culture.

One pioneering brand that showcases the vibrant spirit of Mexico is Quiquiriqui, named after the Spanish version of 'cock-a-doodle-doo'. The hallucinatory label images were created by Mexico City designer Ese, who apparently had the underside of a mushroom in mind for the abstract shape, in homage to one of Mexico's other magical gifts.

Ese also designed the 5-litre (10½-pint) boxes that Quiquiriqui most recently brought to market. Although at first I questioned the experience of having such a valuable spirit arrive in a box, the reality is an eco-friendly solution to international export. The boxes minimize the carbon footprint by reducing shipping weight and glass production. Customers can use the box to refill bottles, rather than buying new ones.

There is an overlap between premium and artisanal products, but on either side of the Venn diagram, premium brands tend to use darker, often embossed labels on heavyweight bottles. Artisanal brands often lean towards a simple, earthy feel. Sometimes brands will showcase their sustainable ideals by using agave fibre paper and recycled glass bottles. For the artisanal category, there is often the sense of 'discovering' the spirits through filling plastic bottles with the precious liquid.

Madre mezcal has pioneered a particularly earthy aesthetic popular in agave spirits branding, one they have successfully carried through from brand story to bottle. Madre, which means 'mother', honours the land where the mezcal comes from.

The creative journey of Madre began when founder Tony Farfalla travelled to Mexico to learn about the country's history of shamanism and spirituality. Tony fell in love with mezcal and began to bring back plastic bottles of it that he labelled madre. With the support of designer Stefan Weigand, the Madre brand grew into how it is known today. Farfalla states that madre is a simple yet powerful word that resonates with the beauty we find in mezcal. It holds a tie to nature and to the earth that provides us with so many gifts, including mezcal.

BELOW: *Mexican artist Bouler on a walk around Oaxaca City, home to many of his beautiful murals.*

The simple yet evocative branding for Madre conveys the romance of artisanal production while paying tribute to rustic techniques that mezcal makers have relied on for generations. The brand's ideas and style have since been hugely influential on the style associated with contemporary mezcal brands.

Another artist who has sought to preserve their first experiences of mezcal is Guillermo Olguín, co-founder of Los Amantes mezcal. Olguín is a familiar face as he drives around the city of Oaxaca in his battered old Jeep, giving him the air of an old-world explorer. He designed the Los Amantes bottle to reflect the glass demijohns in which mezcaleros store their spirits.

Olguín's aesthetic has also influenced the way mezcalerías look today, with floor to ceiling mezcal, often in unlabelled glass. The original Los Amantes bar is a hole-in-the-wall spot in Oaxaca's historic centre. There are low benches that emulate the experience of sitting at a roadside mezcal spot, and curious found items he describes as amuletos (charms).

In 2013 I spent many a night in Mezcalería Los Amantes, having lock-ins, standing on the tiny bar and singing along to Don Zenon on the guitar. At that time, mezcal expert Leon Langle was the bartender. He would serve you great big jícaras full of mezcal. If you wanted to buy a bottle of Los Amantes, Leon would siphon mezcal from one of the demijohns into a plain glass bottle, then stick on a simple label on which he would write what you had just bought: an experience pretty close to that of buying bottles out at a distillery.

ABOVE: *A 20-litre (42-pint) garrafón (water cooler jug) filled with mezcal. This is a typical way to store mezcal for long periods.*

The sort of thing you would want written on your bottle (especially so you don't make the rookie error of confusing it with water) is 'mezcal' or whichever agave spirit you are collecting, then the type of agave and the alcohol percentage. I usually have the producer sign and date my purchase as well. This always reminds me how each bottle is like a limited-edition artwork. As Guillermo Olguín puts it, 'the palenqueros are artists, and this is the gallery'.

CHOOSING A BOTTLE

If you aren't filling your water bottle with mezcal at a palenque, you are probably in a bar or a liquor store, or perhaps online, looking at buying from the thousands of brands on the market. If so, here are a few more criteria to help guide you towards the right agave spirit for you.

Some (but often not all) of the following details can be found on the label. The aim is to provide the consumer with truthful and comparable information:

1. Brand/producer name
2. Class, such as joven or añejo
3. Agave species/ensemble/any additional elements
4. Alcohol percentage
5. Exact location of production (the name of the community, not just the state)
6. NOM number
7. Date of production and batch number
8. Characteristics of the production process, such as the tools used
9. Tax information
10. QR code to scan for info

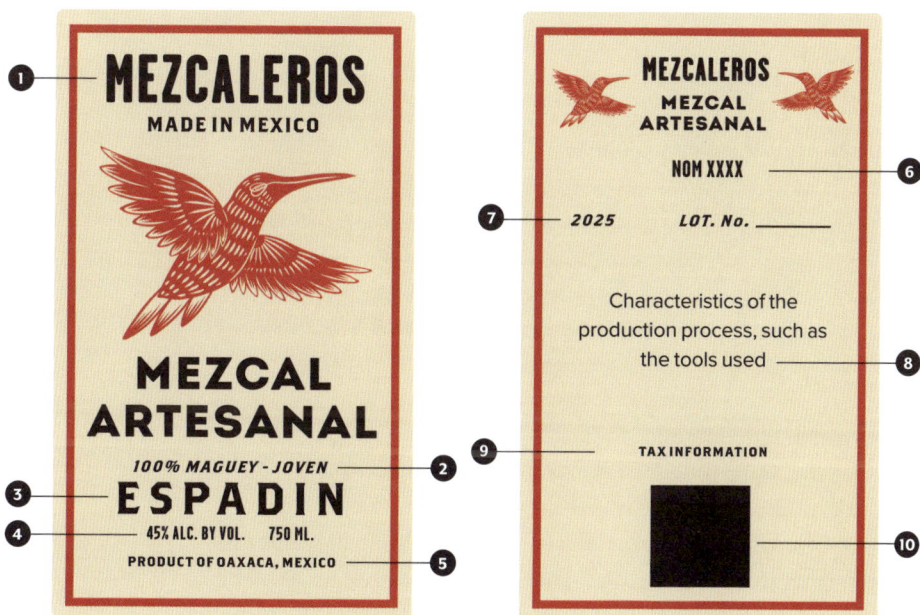

MEZCALEROS
MADE IN MEXICO

MEZCAL
ARTESANAL

100% MAGUEY - JOVEN
ESPADIN
45% ALC. BY VOL.   750 ML.
PRODUCT OF OAXACA, MEXICO

MEZCALEROS
MEZCAL
ARTESANAL

NOM XXXX

2025   LOT. No. _____

Characteristics of the production process, such as the tools used

TAX INFORMATION

HOW TO DRINK AGAVE SPIRITS

Many people will drink agave spirits in the way my British friends might drink tea: a sip whenever it feels right. Many producers I know have a mezcal first thing in the morning or last thing at night, or after finishing a period of hard work. Some say it should be drunk to mark a celebration. Whatever the occasion, the first thing you are told when handed a delicious agave spirit is: sip it, don't shoot it! Whether you are drinking from a terracotta cup, a champagne flute or even just an old plastic water bottle, the liquid should be savoured. The best way to drink agave spirits is with care and respect.

Different agave expressions, terroir, ageing and even the alcohol percentage will all influence the final spirit. The weather, environment and what you have previously tasted may also have an impact on the flavours. For example, if it's a hot, still day, the aromas may be more intense. If it's cold and raining, the flavours will be more subtle.

In an unaged agave spirit you should notice the taste of cooked agave, which usually gives a range of notes, from sweetness, smoke, fruit and nuts to minerality and lactic notes. For anything barrel-aged there will also be caramel, vanilla, chocolate and oak.

Before drinking, it helps to prepare your palate. You can do this by putting a little spirit on exposed skin. Give it a few seconds to allow the alcohol to evaporate, then give it a sniff: it should smell like cooked agave. Doing this will help you pick out those notes when you start to drink.

ABOVE: *Showing the 'legs' of the spirit in a snifter glass. 'Legs' occur when liquids with different surface tensions, such as water and alcohol, flow away from each other.*

Begin by taking a small sip. I like to hold the first sip for a moment, breathing out alcohol fumes through my nose while feeling the texture of the liquid on my tongue. This also allows for the flavours to open up

ABOVE: *Mezcaleros in Ejutla sharing a mezcal in cups made from a type of reed called carrizo.*

more, mixing slightly with your saliva. When you finally swallow the spirit there may be a light burn in the top of your mouth, depending on the agave type and processes involved. There can be a disconnect between alcohol percentage and burn.

A lower-proof spirit will have had water added to bring it down to the desired percentage. Water mixes with the beautiful oils in the agave spirits and makes the texture thinner; this helps it open up as you sip and gives you a burn like the feeling of a strong alcohol. This is usually if the spirit is 42% ABV or lower, such as a mezcal intended for use in cocktails.

A great agave spirit designed for sipping will usually be over 45% ABV. It has the effect of coating your mouth with flavour. The viscosity limits the burn and can actually make the liquid feel like it's less strong, even if it's technically more alcoholic.

There's a special way to sip, and it involves bringing the spirit to your lips and mimicking a little kiss. One of the many sayings from the world of agave spirits is that respect goes both ways: 'Treat it like your lover. Kiss it and it will treat you right. Hit it and it will **** you up.'

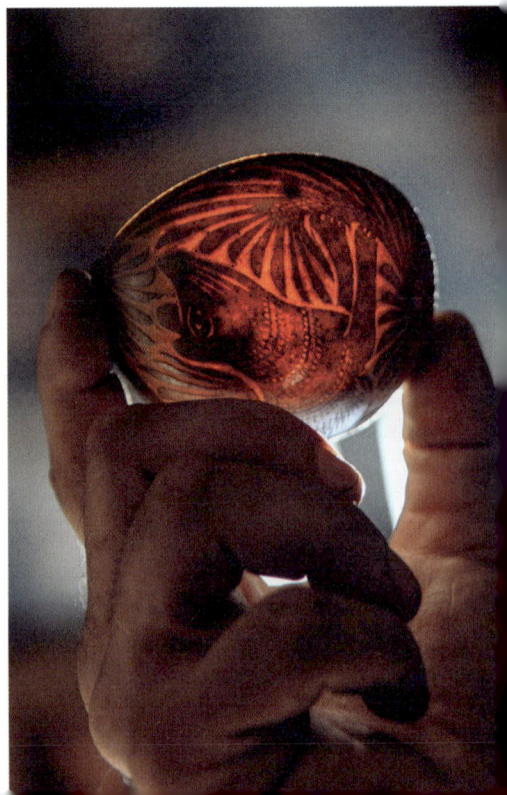

DRINKING VESSELS

For agave spirits, the type of drinking vessel you have available will greatly affect the flavour profile. Traditional wide-mouthed copitas or veladoras that you find in Oaxaca disperse the first hit of alcohol. Traditional tall shot glasses, on the other hand, focus aromas and vapours directly into your nostrils, making a drink seem stronger.

The renowned glassware manufacturer Riedel designed some glasses for tequila with a bowl that tapers towards the nose, allowing the smells to swirl before concentrating them towards the nose as you take a sip.

In Oaxaca, the most common way to drink agave spirits is in a veladora, which is a straight-sided glass with ribbed walls and a cross in the bottom. Some people will tell you that to show your appreciation you should drink until you 'see the cross'. This doesn't mean knocking it back, but rather appreciating every drop down to the last. These final drops are las gotas de felicidad – the 'drops of happiness'.

Agave spirits from the north are often served in tall, slim glasses called caballitos, which means 'little horses'. Some think the glass evolved from a tradition of drinking tequila from a hollowed-out bull's horn, like those used to measure the perlas in sotol. Ordering a caballito would let the bartender know you want it neat, rather than with a side of Coke or other chaser.

These days connoisseurs may use Riedel glasses or champagne flutes to enhance their tasting journey. Using a flute can make the experience more finessed, which is not just about aesthetics: it is good to let the spirit aerate a little to bring out softer, more nuanced flavours. A shot glass can hold only 45ml (1½fl oz) of liquid, whereas a flute can hold about 175ml (6fl oz). The extra space allows the spirit to have more contact with the air, and allows you to swirl it with style.

Aesthetics are important, too, considering how we tend to taste with our eyes first. An elevated experience can help us slow down and appreciate what we are drinking. Passing someone a mezcal in a tasting glass communicates that this is something to be savoured and appreciated. Using an elegant glass shows respect for the time and energy that went into producing the spirit.

OPPOSITE, CLOCKWISE FROM TOP LEFT: *Veladora glasses, originally used as candle holders, are now synonymous with drinking mezcal.*

A decorative clay copita.

A carved jícara catching the light. These gourds are traditionally used for agave spirits.

A Riedel-style glass designed for Don Fulano.

MEZCALERÍAS AND COCKTAILS

Nowadays there are more places than ever offering a range of agave spirits. As interest in the category continues to accelerate, so does the number of agave-centric venues. Although big-brand tequilas have long had a monopoly in bars as cheap pours, in recent years the more artisanal and niche agave spirits have started to populate the shelves of liquor stores, tasting rooms, restaurants, and even the home bar.

Mezcalerías and tasting rooms are environments dedicated to trying agave spirits. They are influenced by the palenque experience, as well as the more established settings of wine bars and whisky tasting rooms. The setting is often relaxed, almost homey. These establishments often have extensive varieties to try from, either stacked impressively like a library of bottles, or a rotating selection to showcase new, unusual pours. Staff are knowledgeable, so they can guide you through a tasting flight (see page 195). They may offer some curated snacks to enjoy with your sips. Pairings with mezcal can be as vast as the portfolio of mezcal itself. The best-known accompaniments for agave spirits are citrus fruit and salt, but cheese, chocolate, salts, fruits and even insects all are great with mezcal, and commonly served. There is an enjoyable ritual to be had in sipping mezcal with a taste of orange and chilli salt. However, if you are looking for nuances in your glass, these snacks can be overwhelming to the palate.

Restaurants may not have the range of an agave-focused tasting room, but they can offer exciting complementary flavours. Food pairings are great with agave spirits, such as a bright espadín with ceviche, or tepeztate with steak; and agave spirits go really well with chocolate too – as if you needed to be told twice! For those with a curious palate, curated pairing menus can represent the peak of culinary exploration. Artistry lies in discerning how specific agave spirits can complement and enhance each course.

Agave spirits have become a firm favourite of mixologists too, and they can add depth, complexity, smoke and brightness to cocktails. There are, of course, some famous cocktails for agave spirits, namely the Tequila Sunrise and the Margarita, or modern classics such as the Mezcal Negroni and Oaxaca Old Fashioned. There are also regional sips such as the Batanga, which is similar to a Cuba Libre and made famous by La Capilla in Tequila.

I love to drink agave spirit cocktails with locally sourced ingredients. London's Kol restaurant has made waves in recent years with its innovative pairings and cocktails using homegrown British ingredients, Mexican techniques and agave spirits. In Oaxaca we are spoiled with the array of fruits, herbs and spices to make an exciting cocktail. Brooks has made moreish Margaritas with homemade árbol chilli salts, sours made with foraged aromatic herbs, and Martinis refreshed with a spray of avocado leaf tincture. He takes guests out to the agave fields to share these drinks on site with producers.

Whatever the premise, as with the notion of pairing food and agave spirits, a great cocktail should have elements that complement and enhance the primary ingredient: agave! Tasting agave spirits is awesome wherever you are – whether that's an agave field, a distillery, a bar or the back of a pick-up truck. The flavours are evocative and transportative, a journey in themselves. It's no surprise that the most exciting venues worldwide are using the medium of agave spirits to transport their guests.

BELOW: *Cantina La Capilla, the oldest bar in Tequila. Established in 1940 by Don Javier Delgado Corona, his creation, the Batanga cocktail, has gained international fame. It's a mix of tequila, cola, lime juice and a pinch of salt, stirred with a long knife.*

FLIGHTS AND COCKTAILS

AGAVE SPIRIT FLIGHTS

Tasting flights are a great way to dive deeper into the agave spirits category. They elevate the story of the spirit, and help to start a conversation around the different varieties. In this context, the term 'flight' is used to describe a selection of agave spirits served in a considered series that will take you on a journey through taste. Although you can use great spirits in a cocktail, some of the nuance will be lost in the citrus and sugar. Choosing a single spirit to try can be a challenge and an investment: there are some amazing rare options, but they tend to be correspondingly expensive.

A flight is a way to sample different agave spirits without ordering full pours or bottles. They usually consist of three to five servings, with only a small amount for tasting, between 15–30ml (½–1fl oz), depending on who is pouring!

The possibilities for flights are boundless due to the diversity of agave, styles of process and brands. Successful flights typically start with a concept, which could be a range of agave varieties from a single producer, a particular region, a distillation style or even the vessel you drink it from. Ideally, other variables will be limited, aside from the concept of the flight.

OPPOSITE: *¡Salud! Bar owner Miguel Martínez Cruz raises a glass during a cocktail tasting with Brooks Bailey at Bar Ilegales in Oaxaca.*

A flight will often flow from a classic or simple taste profile to something richer, more complex and challenging. For example, in an espadín mezcal flight tends to be simple and sweet. Starting there and moving through agave varieties based on increasing maturity, you would expect the notes to become more complex and 'funky'.

There are some great projects and clubs built around the concept of flights, including Maguey Melate and Sin Gusano. They send out regular selections to be tried with their suggested tasting notes, often including an option to engage with other enthusiasts through guided discussions online.

If you enjoy agave spirits but have never tried flights before, the best thing is to jump in and get started. You'll find out whether you prefer bold, complex or smooth flavours as you continue your journey through agave spirits. Although there are great snacks and pairings to go alongside, I would suggest sipping only water between sips of a flight to keep the palate clean and refreshed. I have included a flight based on vessel style, but normally I suggest using glass cups, as they will be most neutral.

BELOW: *A flight (themed selection) of agave spirits.*

FLIGHT SUGGESTIONS

CURATED BY BROOKS BAILEY

THE PROCESS

1. Swirl the liquid gently in the glass. Notice the viscosity of the liquid as 'legs' that run down the side of the glass. Take in the aromas. Note any scents such as fruit, spice or oak.

2. Taste mindfully. Take a small sip and let it coat your palate. Pay attention to the flavours, the mouthfeel and the finish.

3. Discuss and compare. Encourage open discussion among your guests. Everyone's palate is different, and sharing impressions can be enlightening. Make sure to sip water between tastes to refresh your palate and stay hydrated.

CLASSIC OAXACA SPECIES ARTISANAL FLIGHT FROM MEZCAL SALVADORES

Designed to taste species from the quickest to mature to the longest to mature.
All produced in Tlacolula, Oaxaca, at the Palacios distillery.

1 ▷ **2** ▷ **3** ▷ **4**

Agave espadín, **6–10 years (47% ABV)**	**Agave tobalá,** **12–15 years (48% ABV)**	**Agave cirial,** **15–18 years (48% ABV)**	**Agave tepeztate,** **15–30+years (48% ABV)**
Notes: sweet, light molasses, grass, green apple	Notes: floral, fruity, hint of caramel	Notes: wood, heavy minerality, pine	Notes: fresh-cut green peppers, jalapeño, brine

---

PRIMOS FLIGHT

Designed to showcase iconic agave spirit categories, side by side.

1 ▷ **2** ▷ **3** ▷ **4**

Mezcal: **Salvadores Espadín**	**Bacanora:** **Santo Cuviso**	**Raicilla:** **El Viaje**	**Sotol:** **Hacienda de** **Chihuahua Plata**
Notes: crisp, fresh, green apple, cooked agave	Notes: honeysuckle, minty minerality, very dry finish	Notes: bright citrus, creamy vanilla, earth, vegetal	Notes: mint, green, vegetal

TEQUILANA FLIGHT

Designed to taste *Agave tequilana* distillates from different states.

① ▷ **②** ▷ **③** ▷ **④**

Fortaleza Blanco (40% ABV)
Tequila, Jalisco
Notes: citrus, cooked agave, vanilla, basil, olive, lime

Cascahuin Plata (48% ABV)
Arenal area, Jalisco
Notes: agave, black pepper, vanilla, mint, citrus

Derrumbes Zacatecas, Joven tequilana Weber (48% ABV),
Hacienda de Guadalupe, Zacatecas
Notes: dry grass, wet clay, rubber and black pepper

Real Minero Agave tequilana Weber (53.4% ABV)
Central Valleys, Oaxaca
Notes: white pepper, honeysuckle, light chocolate, damp soil

AGED TEQUILA FLIGHT

Designed to showcase tequila unaged and aged for differing times in barrel.

① ▷ **②** ▷ **③**

Don Fulano Blanco (40% ABV)
Notes: bright, lively, floral, light herbaceousness

Reposado, 8–11 months (40% ABV)
Notes: round on the palate, coconut, macadamia

Añejo, 30 months minimum (40% ABV)
Notes: baked banana, tropical citrus, dried harvest fruit

ALIPÚS SINGLE-VILLAGE MEZCAL FLIGHT

Designed to offer expressions from different towns in the central valleys of Oaxaca, to show the terroir and varying styles of each town.

Santa Ana del Rio
Notes: summer melons, chalk, grilled smoky herbs, mineral

San Juan
Notes: fruit, rich, smoke, sweet

① ▷ **②** ▷

⑤ ◁ **④** ◁ **③**

San Luis del Rio
Notes: saline, chilli pepper, cashew, fruit

San Baltazar Guelavila
Notes: citrus, rich cooked agave, banana

San Andres
Notes: fruit forward, sweet, cooked agave

DRINKING VESSEL FLIGHT

Designed to offer the same spirit in different vessels to taste how it express differently from each one.

1 ▷ **2** ▷ **3**

Jícara
(dried fruit of the calabash [*Crescentia cujete*] tree), unpainted

Clay copita
Glazed and unglazed will have different expressions

Glass
Clean, pure expression

TEQUILA BLANCO FLIGHT

Designed to showcase unaged (blanco) tequila from different brands.

1 ▷ **2** ▷ **3** ▷ **4**

Fortaleza Still Strength Blanco (46% ABV)
Notes: vegetal fruit, fully ripened agave, green olive, earth, black pepper

Don Fulano Blanco Fuerte 100 (50% ABV)
Notes: aromatic, floral, jasmine, orange blossom

Arette Fuerte 101 Blanco (50.5% ABV)
Notes: earth, light smoke, spice, pepper, anise, honey, hint of citrus

Tequila Ocho Puntas Plata 101 (50.5% ABV)
Notes: white pepper, salt water, citrus, cinnamon, anise, saline minerality

DERRUMBES STATE-BY-STATE MEZCAL FLIGHT

Designed to taste Derrumbes expressions from different Mezcal-producing states, to show the terroir and varying styles of each state.

Oaxaca: Espadín / Tobalá (48% ABV)
Notes: fresh citrus, pine, rich cooked agave, light smoke

Durango: Joven Durangensis (45% ABV)
Notes: fruit, soft berries, sweet citrus zest, baked stone

San Luis Potosí: Joven Salmiana Crassispina (43% ABV)
Notes: cooked agave, sweet spices, smoked pepper, sweet, fruit

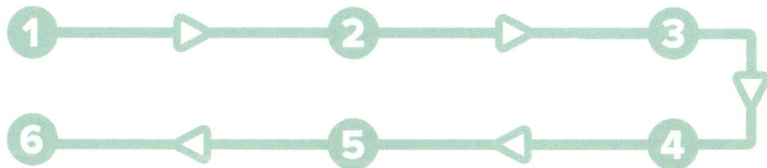

1 ▷ **2** ▷ **3**
              ▽
6 ◁ **5** ◁ **4**

Tamaulipas: Joven Funkiana / Univittata / Americana (46% ABV)
Notes: chocolate, citrus, dry, cherries, crisp minerality

Zacatecas: Joven Tequilana Weber (48% ABV)
Notes: dry grass, wet clay, rubber, black pepper

Michoacán: Joven Cupreata / Alta (45% ABV)
Notes: woody leather, vegetal spice, slightly lactic

COCKTAILS

DESIGNED BY BROOKS BAILEY

Brooks Bailey began his bartending career in 2012 as part of the opening
bar crew at Comal in Berkeley, California, where he learned from Bay Area
bartenders Scott Baird, Michael Carlisi and Matthew Campbell. Now
Brooks lives in Oaxaca, where he works with different mezcaleros and
local bars.

My most inspiring moments come from many hours spent with
mezcaleros. Some of my favourite mezcaleros have an affinity for
their destilados con, and this has often been the start of some of
my more creative cocktails. From tobacco (Noble Coyote), to coffee
(Dangerous Don), to marigold (Salvadores), no matter the flavour,
something from the mezcalero inspires the impetus for a cocktail.
It feels like a collaboration.

When developing cocktails for agave spirits, it is important to showcase
the nuances of the spirit and not smother them. An easy rule of thumb
is to replace mezcal for gin: we have yet to find a gin cocktail that is not
enhanced by substituting with mezcal.

One of Brooks' go-to cocktails is a 2–1–½ Margarita made with
mezcal, lime and simple sugar syrup. You could make a special salt,
a syrup, a juice, a tincture…maybe an ice cube made with black tea
and lemon zest frozen within.

You can find instructions for making the salts, syrups, infusions and
ice cubes on page 214–17.

OPPOSITE: *Rambling Spirits founder Brooks Bailey at*
Bar Ilegales in Oaxaca.

MEZCAL MARGARITA

60ml (2fl oz) mezcal

30ml (1fl oz) lime juice

15ml (½fl oz) simple sugar syrup
  or agave syrup (see page 214)

salt, orange bitters and lime slice, to garnish

Shake the first three ingredients with ice, strain over ice cubes into a rocks glass half-rimmed with salt. Garnish with a lime slice. Add several dashes of orange bitters if you're missing the Triple Sec in a classic Margarita.

TAUGHT HOTTIE

60ml (2fl oz) espadín mezcal

15ml (½fl oz) ginger syrup (see page 215)

15ml (½fl oz) chamomile syrup (see page 215)

22ml (¾fl oz) lemon juice

lemon slice and whole cloves, to garnish

Combine all the ingredients in a prewarmed mug, top with hot water and garnish with a lemon slice studded with cloves.

PIRUL-OMA

60ml (2fl oz) espadín mezcal

30ml (1fl oz) grapefruit juice

15ml (½fl oz) pink peppercorn syrup
  (see page 215)

8ml (¼fl oz) lime juice

soda water, to taste

pink peppercorn salt and grapefruit slice,
  to garnish

Shake the first four ingredients with ice, strain over ice cubes into a rocks glass half-rimmed with pink peppercorn salt. Add a splash of soda and garnish with a half-moon slice of grapefruit.

ZAPOTIKI

45ml (1½fl oz) espadín mezcal

22ml (¾fl oz) pineapple juice

15ml (½fl oz) Luxardo Maraschino liqueur

8ml (¼fl oz) lime juice

8ml (¼fl oz) agave syrup (see page 214)

salt, to garnish

dark rum, to taste

Shake the first five ingredients with ice, then strain over ice cubes into a glass rimmed with salt (I use sal de chapulin, aka grasshopper salt). Gently pour a little dark rum to float on top.

OPPOSITE: *Mezcal Margarita*

ROCÍO DE MONTAÑA

60ml (2fl oz) espadín mezcal
22ml (¾fl oz) lemongrass syrup (see page 214)
15ml (½fl oz) dry vermouth
8ml (¼fl oz) lime juice
soda water, to taste
avocado leaf bitters (see page 216)

Shake the first four ingredients with ice, then strain over ice cubes into a glass. Add a splash of soda and five dashes of avocado leaf bitters.

LAZY DELIRIUM

60ml (2fl oz) sotol
15ml (½fl oz) chamomile syrup (see page 215)
15ml (½fl oz) dry vermouth
soda water, to taste
cinnamon bitters (see page 216)
lime peel twist and cinnamon stick, to garnish

Pour the first three ingredients over ice into a rocks glass and stir. Add a splash of soda and three dashes of cinnamon bitters. Garnish with a lime peel twist and cinnamon stick.

JALA-PIÑA

45ml (1½fl oz) espadín mezcal
30ml (1fl oz) pineapple juice
30ml (1fl oz) jalapeño syrup (see page 215)
15ml (½fl oz) dry vermouth
8ml (¼fl oz) lime juice
2 dashes spicy tincture (see page 216)
jalapeño salt, to garnish (see page 214)

Shake the first six ingredients with ice and strain over ice cubes into a rocks glass half-rimmed with jalapeño salt.

TOMACCO

60 ml (2fl oz) tobacco leaf-infused mezcal (such as Noble Coyote)
30 ml (1fl oz) tomato-raspberry syrup (see page 215)
15 ml (½fl oz) lime juice
15 ml (½fl oz) dry vermouth
soda water, to taste
lime wheel, to garnish

Shake the first four ingredients with ice, then strain over ice cubes into a rocks glass. Add a splash of soda and garnish with a lime wheel.

OPPOSITE: *Lazy Delirium*

CAMPORIÑA

½ lime, quartered
2 teaspoons sugar
60ml (2fl oz) sotol
sage leaf, to garnish

Muddle the lime wedges and sugar in
a rocks glass, then add the sotol and
stir. Fill with crushed ice and stir again.
Garnish with a sage leaf.

BACK TO THE ROOTS

60ml (2fl oz) espadín mezcal or tequila blanco
22ml (¾fl oz) beetroot juice
30ml (1fl oz) ginger syrup (see page 215)
cracked black pepper and rock salt, to garnish

Shake the first three ingredients with ice,
then strain over ice cubes into a rocks
glass half-rimmed with cracked black
pepper and rock salt.

MEXICANO

30ml (1fl oz) coffee-infused mezcal (see page 217)
22ml (¾fl oz) Campari
30ml (1fl oz) sweet vermouth
soda water
lemon twist and coffee beans, to garnish

Fill a glass with ice and pour in the first
three ingredients. Top with soda water
and gently stir. Garnish with a lemon twist
and 3 coffee beans.

SANTA ORIA

45ml (1½fl oz) espadín mezcal
22ml (¾fl oz) carrot juice
15ml (½fl oz) lemon juice
22ml (¾fl oz) chamomile syrup (see page 215)
soda water
parsley sprig, to garnish

Shake the first four ingredients with ice,
then strain over ice cubes into a 250ml
(8fl oz) glass. Top up with soda water and
garnish with a parsley sprig.

OPPOSITE: *Camporiña*

MEZCAL MULE

60ml (2fl oz) espadín mezcal
30ml (1fl oz) lime juice
30ml (1fl oz) ginger syrup
soda water, to taste
Angostura Bitters or mole bitters (see page 216),
   to taste
lime wheel, to garnish

Shake the first three ingredients with ice, then strain over ice cubes into copper mule mug or tall tumbler. Add a splash of soda and several dashes of bitters, then garnish with a lime wheel.

DESERT MARTINI
(RAICILLA DIRTY OLD MARTINI)

60ml (2fl oz) raicilla
30ml (1fl oz) dry vermouth
dirty ice cube (see page 216)
pearl onion, olive and sage leaf skewer,
   to garnish (optional)

Stir the raicilla and vermouth together, then strain over a large dirty ice cube into a martini or rocks glass. Garnish with a pearl onion, olive and sage leaf skewer, if you like.

AGAVE OLD FASHIONED

30ml (1fl oz) espadín mezcal
30ml (1fl oz) reposado tequila
15ml (½fl oz) simple sugar syrup (see page 216)
2 dashes Angostura Bitters
3 dashes mole bitters (see page 216)
lemon and orange zest, to garnish

Stir the first five ingredients with ice, then pour over a large ice cube into a rocks glass. Garnish with lemon and orange zest.

BEDLAMITE

22ml (¾fl oz) raicilla
22ml (¾fl oz) Green Chartreuse
22ml (¾fl oz) sweet vermouth
lemon peel twist, to garnish

Stir the first three ingredients with ice, then strain into a chilled Nick & Nora glass or other small-stemmed cocktail glass. Garnish with a lemon peel twist.

OPPOSITE: *Desert Martini*

SONORA SUNRISE

60ml (2fl oz) bacanora
30ml (1fl oz) mango juice
30ml (1fl oz) pineapple juice
2 dashes Angostura Bitters
15ml (½fl oz) Aperol
dehydrated citrus wheel, to garnish

Shake the first three ingredients with ice.
Add the Angostura Bitters to a tall glass,
fill the glass with ice and add the Aperol.
Double-strain the bacanora and fruit juices
over the Aperol (without disturbing it) and
garnish with a dehydrated citrus wheel.

BELL PEPPER MARGARITA

60ml (2fl oz) tequila blanco
30ml (1fl oz) bell pepper syrup (see page 215)
15ml (½fl oz) lime juice

Prepare a rocks glass with a Spicy, Sweet
and Sour rim (see page 214). Shake all the
cocktail ingredients with ice, then strain
over ice cubes into the rocks glass.

PALOMA

45ml (1½fl oz) tequila blanco
45ml (1½fl oz) grapefruit juice
15ml (½fl oz) dry vermouth
15ml (½fl oz) simple or honey syrup (see page 214)
8ml (¼fl oz) lime juice
soda water, to taste
salt, grapefruit zest and fresh rosemary sprig,
    to garnish

Shake the first five ingredients with ice,
strain into a tall glass half-rimmed with
salt. Add a splash of soda and garnish
with grapefruit zest and a rosemary sprig.

PEPINO COOLER

45ml (1½fl oz) espadín mezcal
15ml (½fl oz) mint mezcal
30ml (1fl oz) cucumber syrup (see page 215)
8ml (¼fl oz) dry vermouth
8ml (¼fl oz) lime juice
soda water, to taste
cucumber strip, to garnish

Shake the first five ingredients with ice,
then strain over ice cubes into a tall glass.
Add a splash of soda, then garnish with
a cucumber strip.

OPPOSITE: *Sonora Sunrise*

NAKED AND FAMOUS AND SOUR

22ml (¾fl oz) espadín mezcal
22ml (¾fl oz) Aperol
22ml (¾fl oz) Yellow Chartreuse
22ml (¾fl oz) lemon juice
1 egg white

Combine all the ingredients and shake without ice. Now add ice and shake again, then double-strain into a champagne saucer (coupe glass).

PSYCHOPOMP

30ml (1fl oz) Dangerous Don coffee
    espadín mezcal (see page 118),
    or coffee-infused mezcal (see page 217)
22ml (¾fl oz) sweet vermouth
22ml (¾fl oz) Campari
orange peel twist, to garnish (optional)

Stir the first four ingredients together, then pour into a glass over a large ice cube with a marigold frozen inside (see page 216). Garnish with orange peel twist, if you like.

AL PASTOR

45ml (1½fl oz) espadín mezcal
45ml (1½fl oz) piña-guajillo syrup (see page 215)
8ml (¼fl oz) lime juice
soda water, to taste
salt and pineapple slice and leaf, to garnish

Shake the first three ingredients with ice, then strain over ice cubes into a tall glass rimmed with salt (I use Tajin or sal de chapulin). Add a splash of soda and garnish with a pineapple slice and leaf.

CABALLERO

30ml (1fl oz) tobacco leaf-infused mezcal
    (such as Noble Coyote)
30ml (1fl oz) raicilla
15ml (½fl oz) guajillo syrup (see page 215)
2 dashes Angostura Bitters
flamed orange peel, to garnish

Stir the first four ingredients with ice, then double-strain over a large ice cube into a rocks glass. Garnish with flamed orange peel.

OPPOSITE: *Psychopomp*

SALTS, RIMS AND POWDERS

A rim is a visual and flavourful way to personalize a cocktail. The suggested combinations below – of zest, spices, citric acid, salt and sugar – will supplement or complement the accompanying cocktails.

ANGOSTURA SUGAR: Spread 250g (9oz) demerara sugar onto a baking sheet, add 10–12 dashes Angostura Bitters and leave to dry/dehydrate. Mix well to combine.

LIME ZEST SALT: Zest 10 limes and dehydrate the zest. Blend it into a powder and mix with the salt of your choice.

GRAPEFRUIT ZEST SALT: Zest 10 grapefruits and dehydrate the zest. Blend it into a powder and mix with the salt of your choice.

PINK PEPPERCORN SALT: Toast pink peppercorns, blend into a powder and mix with the salt of your choice

JALAPEÑO SALT: Deseed 500g (1lb 2oz) jalapeños, dice the flesh and leave to dehydrate. Grind into a powder and mix with the salt of your choice.

SPICY, SWEET AND SOUR RIM: Take 2 dried arból chillies, 1 teaspoon citric acid and 2 tablespoons sugar and blend into a powder.

COOKED SYRUPS

Teas, herbs, flowers, spices and many types of fruit impart great flavour when cooked into a syrup.

SIMPLE SYRUP: Heat equal quantities of hot water and sugar, stir then allow to cool.

HONEY SYRUP: Heat equal quantities of hot water and honey, stir then allow to cool.

AGAVE SYRUP: Heat equal quantities of hot water and agave syrup, stir then allow to cool.

ABOVE: *Honey Syrup*

PINK PEPPERCORN SYRUP: Toast 500g (18oz) pink peppercorns in a pan, add to 500ml (18fl oz) boiling water and let steep. Blend, strain and measure, then add an equal volume of sugar.

GUAJILLO SYRUP: Put 500g (18oz) deseeded guajillo chillies in a pan with 2 litres (3½ pints) water and bring to the boil. Once boiling, simmer until reduced to 1 litre (1¾ pints). Strain and measure, then add 500g (18oz) sugar.

PIÑA-GUAJILLO SYRUP: Toast 300g (10½oz) deseeded guajillo chillies in a pan. Add 2 litres (3½ pints) pineapple juice, bring to the boil and simmer until reduced to 1 litre (1¾ pints). Strain and add 500g (18oz) sugar.

JAMAICA SYRUP: Put 100g (3½oz) dried hibiscus flowers in a pan with 1 litre (1¾ pints) pineapple juice, 4 cinnamon sticks and 2 arból chillies. Bring to the boil and simmer for 20–30 minutes, then strain and measure. Add an equal volume of sugar.

CHAMOMILE SYRUP: Steep 2 bunches fresh chamomile or 100g (3½oz) dried chamomile in 1 litre (1¾ pints) boiling water, covered, for 20 minutes. Once cool, strain and add an equal volume of sugar.

GINGER SYRUP: Blend 2kg (4lb 8oz) fresh ginger with 500ml (18fl oz) water, then strain, reserving the juice. Add the pulp to a large pan with 1.2 litres (2 pints) water. Bring to the boil, then simmer for 20 minutes. Turn off the heat and leave to cool. Strain and combine the liquid with the reserved juice. Measure and add half as much sugar as liquid.

TOMATO-RASPBERRY SYRUP: Blister 1kg (2lb 4oz) cherry tomatoes in a pan. Add 500g (1lb 2oz) frozen raspberries, stir and leave to soften. Heat to a simmer, then strain. Add 400g (14oz) sugar.

COLD MACERATION

This is a great way to highlight the vegetal aspects of ingredients. A ratio of 1:1 sugar and liquid is good, but to add extra flavour add 2 parts liquid to 1 part sugar. This means you can make twice the amount of syrup without adding too much sweetness.

JALAPEÑO SYRUP: Deseed 500g (18oz) green jalapeños, blend with 400ml (14fl oz) water, then strain and measure. Add half the amount of sugar to liquid.

CUCUMBER SYRUP: Juice 3 cucumbers and add half the amount of sugar to liquid.

LEMONGRASS SYRUP: Blend finely sliced fresh lemongrass with 400ml (14fl oz) water. Strain and add an equal volume of sugar.

BELL PEPPER SYRUP: Blend 3kg (7lb) red bell peppers with 500ml (18fl oz) water then strain and measure. Add half the amount of sugar to liquid.

ICE CUBES/ROCKS

Often overlooked, ice cubes frozen with added flavours are an easy way to fancy up a simple cocktail – or if you're out and about, the flavoured ice itself could be your cocktail. Tea ice cubes look and taste nice, while cubes frozen with edible flowers or orange and lemon slices are great for your house party punch. Or try a large dirty cube for a Desert Martini (see page 208).

DIRTY ROCK: Freeze ⅔ water to ⅓ olive brine, or use half and half. Fancy up the rocks with an olive, pearl onion or sage leaf.

THYME ROCK: Infuse a thyme sprig in hot water and leave to cool. Strain and freeze the liquid.

ABOVE: *A dirty rock ice cube.*

BITTERS, TINCTURES AND INFUSIONS

Consisting of alcohol and aromatics, these can be used to add flavour to a cocktail. The main difference between a bitter, tincture and infusion is the concentration of alcohol.

CINNAMON BITTERS: Infuse 5 cinnamon sticks with 200ml (7fl oz) overproof neutral grain spirit for several days, or until it tastes to your liking. Strain, bottle and label.

MOLE BITTERS: Steep 2 ancho chillies, 30g (1oz) bittersweet chocolate (60% cocoa solids) and a cinnamon stick with 200ml (7fl oz) overproof neutral grain spirit for several days, or until it tastes to your liking. Strain, bottle and label.

ORANGE BITTERS: Zest 5 oranges and steep the zest with 200ml (7fl oz) overproof neutral grain spirit several days, or until it tastes to your liking. Strain, bottle and label.

AVOCADO LEAF BITTERS: Fill a jar with avocado leaves and 200ml (7fl oz) overproof neutral grain spirit and leave to infuse for several days, or until it tastes to your liking. Strain, bottle and label.

SPICY TINCTURE: Fill a jar with different types of chillies (a mix of dried and fresh will give your tincture a rounder palate). Arból, guajillo, chipotle and habañero, are good ones to use. Add 200ml (7fl oz) overproof neutral grain spirit and infuse for several days, or until it tastes to your liking. Strain, bottle and label.

COFFEE-INFUSED MEZCAL: Place 500ml (18fl oz) espadín mezcal, 200g (7oz) whole coffee beans and 3 cinnamon sticks in an airtight container. Infuse for an hour, or until it tastes to your liking. Strain, bottle and label.

SANGRITAS

When I find a delicious mezcal that I wouldn't dare put into a cocktail, designing a sangrita to go with that mezcal is always fun. Sangritas are sipping drinks, generally non-alcoholic and made with juices and spices. Traditionally served alongside agave spirits, typically green for blancos and red for aged, they are meant to cleanse the palate and complement the spirit's flavours.

ESPADÍN: Green apples, agave syrup, pineapple juice.

TOBALÁ: Raspberries, cherry tomatoes, cinnamon.

KARWINSKII: Carrot juice, pineapple/ guajillo, cardamom.

TEPEZTATE: Cucumber, grilled pineapple, jalapeño, caper brine.

ABOVE: *Sangritas designed by Brooks Bailey to complement four different expressions of Salvadores mezcal.*

GLOSSARY

ABV: Alcohol by volume

ABOCADO: Mezcal with additional flavours, such as a worm, fruits or herbs

AGAVE: A plant and the raw material for agave spirits

AGUAMIEL: Sweet sap harvested from the heart of an agave; the base liquid for pulque

ALEMBIC: A type of still derived from a 2nd-century Arabic design

ANGELS' SHARE: The liquid that evaporates while ageing alcohol in barrels

BACANORA: A DO-protected agave spirit from Sonora; historically a type of mezcal

BAGASO: Fibres left over after processing agave

BARRANCOS: Underground reservoirs used for storing bacanora

BOTANA: A snack

BONETE: A tree whose hollow trunk is used as the evaporation and condensation chamber in some Filipino-style stills (see page 153)

CABALLITO: A tall shot glass

CANOA: A hollow tree trunk in which cooked agave is mashed with mallets; it may also be used for fermenting cooked agave

CAMPESINO: A farmer/field worker

CAPÓN: An agave left to accumulate sugar after its quiote has been removed

CARRIZO: A plant, a bit like bamboo, used in mezcal production

COA: A circular axe used for harvesting agave

COLAS: The last part of the distillate coming out of the still; low in ethanol, high in methanol

COMITECO: A regional spirit from Chiapas distilled from aguamiel

COPITA: A small cup used for mezcal

CUERPO: The middle part/body of the distillate as it comes out of the still

CURADO: Mezcal or pulque infused with herbs or fruits

DAMAJUANA: A glass or clay vessel for holding mezcal

DO: Denomination of Origin, a classification that protects regional products made using traditional practices

DIXEEBE: A Zapotec term for respect and gratitude, often said in place of 'cheers' when sharing a drink

FÁBRICA: A mezcal production facility

FLIGHT: A selection of agave spirits served in a curated series

FURFURAL: An unwanted, naturally occurring chemical compound created during the agave cooking process, poisonous to humans in large amounts

HORNOS: Earth or stone-lined pit ovens used for cooking agave

INULIN: A prebiotic of fructans present in the roots of various plants

JÍCARA: A dried gourd used as a cup

JIMADOR: A person who harvests agave

MAGUEY: Another name for agave

MAGUEYERO: A person who grows and harvests agave

MAMPOSTERÍA: A steam oven for cooking agave

METL: Another name for gave

MEZCAL: The historical name for most agave spirits in Mexico

MEZCALERÍA: A place to drink mezcal

MIXTO: Tequila made from less than 100 per cent agave

NAHUATL: The language of the Nahua people, known informally as Aztec

NOM: Norma Oficial Mexicana – Mexican government-sanctioned standards/rules for production

ORDINARIO: Liquid produced after a single distillation, also called shishe

PALENQUE: The name for a mezcal production site, often adjacent to a family home; a term commonly used in Oaxaca

PECHUGA: Celebratory mezcal made by adding extra elements to the still; a protein (often meat) is typically suspended in the still to act as a filter

PERLAS: Bubbles formed on the surface of mezcal when the liquid is disturbed; they can be used to assess the ABV

PETATE: Woven palm mat, used to cover a tina

PIÑA: The heart of an agave plant

PRODUCTION: A site that includes land and all the facilities for making agave spirits

PROOF: The measure of alcohol content in a spirit

PULQUE: A drink made from fermented agave sap

PUNTAS: The first part of the distillation process, high ABV

QUIOTE: The flowering stem of an agave

RAICILLA: A DO-protected agave spirit from Jalisco; historically a type of mezcal

REFRESCADERA: A distillation device that can allow for a single distillation

SAL DE GUSANO: A salt made from crushed dried gusano (worm) and chilli

SILVESTRE: Wild agave

SOTOL: A Mexican spirit made from a desert plant called sotol; culturally similar to mezcal and made using a similar process

TABERNA: Site of mezcal production

TAHONA: A large stone wheel pulled by a horse or an ox and used to crush cooked agave

TEPACHE: A fermented liquid made from fruit husks, such as pineapple; also the term for the fermenting mash of cooked agave

TEQUILA: A DO-protected agave spirit; historically known as mezcal

TERROIR: The complete natural environment in which a particular product is produced, including factors such as the soil, topography and climate

TLACHIQUEROS: Pulque farmers

TREN: A type of still used for bacanora; consisting of two oil drums, one acting as the pot and the other as the condenser

TUMBAS: Fermentation vats used for producing sotol

VELADORA: A small glass candle holder often used as a vessel for drinking mezcal

VENENCIA: A straw used by a mezcalero to test the ABV of an agave spirit

VINATA: A distillery where mezcal is produced

VINATERO: A sotol distillery

VINAZA: The liquid waste left in the bottom of the still after the first distillation of agave spirit

ZAPOTEC: Indigenous people from Oaxaca and a Mesoamerican language family

INDEX

FURTHER RESOURCES

BOOKS

Agave Spirits: The Past, Present, and Future of Mezcals by David Suro Pinera and Gary Paul Nabhan (W. W. Norton & Company, 2023)

Divided Spirits: Tequila, Mezcal, and the Politics of Production by Sara Bowen (University of California Press, 2015)

Mezcal: The History, Craft & Cocktails of the World's Ultimate Artisanal Spirit by Emma Janzen (Voyageur Press, 2017)

Perros y Palenques/Distillery Dogs compiled by Anna Bruce

Tequila: A Global History by Ian Williams (Reaktion Books, 2015)

The Essential Tequila & Mezcal Companion by Tessa Rose Lampert (Union Square & Co., 2023)

The Mezcal Experience: A Field Guide to the World's Best Mezcals and Agave Spirits by Tom Bullock (Jacqui Small, 2017)

The Tequila Dictionary by Eric Zandona (Mitchell Beazley, 2019)

Understanding Mezcal by James Schroeder (Prensa Press, 2018)

WEBSITES

Experience Agave, *www.experienceagave.com*

Flaviar, *www.flaviar.com*

Mezcalistas, *www.mezcalistas.com*

Mezcal Reviews, *www.mezcalreviews.com*

Punch, *www.punchdrink.com*

Rambling Spirits, *www.ramblingspirits.com*

PODCASTS

Agave Road Trip by Lou Bank

Heritage Mezcal by Chava Periban and Roy Sierra

ACKNOWLEDGMENTS

This project has only been possible thanks to my ongoing relationships with amazing people from the world of agave. To my friends, family and all those who have guided me to this point, I am beyond grateful.

I am so honoured to have been welcomed by producers, who have trusted me with their knowledge and experience, and also shared many delicious meals and mezcals over the years. Thank you to each brand that has worked with me: getting to know your spirits and the story behind them has been a joy.

I particularly want to mention: Santiago Espinosa de los Monteros Hernández of El Mero Mero, who invited me to my first distillery visit; Hector Audifredd, Leon Langle and David Castillo for welcoming me so warmly into the social scene of Oaxaca; and the creative community in the city for collaborating with me over the years. An extra special thanks to Bouler for his beautiful contributions to this book.

Thank you to the UK mezcal crew who have been a big part of this journey with me. A particular shout-out to Tom Bartram, for letting me tag along on a major trip with him to Mexico, where his passion for agave spirits was inspiring. It was also a chance to meet the incredible team behind Derrumbes mezcal, Esteban Morales and Sergio Mendoza. Graciela Ángeles Carreño of Real Minero has also been beyond generous with her time and deep knowledge about agave spirits in Mexico.

Thank you to Brooks and the bartenders I have had the pleasure of sipping with; your commitment to this complex spirit has helped me understand a whole other side of this story.

Big appreciation to *Mezcalistas* founder Susan Coss, for offering such a supportive platform and open door to ever deeper dives into themes around agave spirits.

I couldn't have gotten this far without the support of the Mexican Embassy in the UK and the SRE (Secretaría de Relaciones Exteriores), who facilitated my first trip to learn about agave spirits and my earliest exhibitions of photography based on this subject.

And last but not least, to Jeannie, Scarlet, Juliette and the team at Octopus Books for their dedication to this project. I have learned so much with you. Thank you!

ABOUT THE AUTHOR

Anna Bruce is a journalist and photographer specializing in the world of agave spirits. Since completing a project looking at the rise of mezcal for the Mexican Foreign Ministry in 2013, she has continued to work regularly for publications focused on agave spirits. These include *Perros y Palenques* and *The Mezcal Experience*, digital content for *Sunset, Culture Trip, Hemisphere Magazine, Food & Wine, Mexico News Daily* and regular contributions to *Mezcalistas*.

Her agave photography has been exhibited at venues such as the V&A, LSE and the Mexican Embassy in London. Currently she is based in Oaxaca with her husband Brooks and six rescue dogs. Together they lead mezcal experiences with Rambling Spirits.

A NOTE ON BRANDS

Every brand I mention in the book has a broader story and context, and most offer numerous expressions of their spirits. Lately, tequila brands have released mezcals and vice versa. The brands featured in this book are very much just a jumping-off point – there are many other brands available. I am sharing just a few examples, with details such as the location, style and flavours of each, along with an approximate price point (the prices may change depending on where you source your agave spirits).

Tasting notes are subjective and influenced by personal experience. Expressions can also be limited in edition, so tasting notes may change over time and with each new batch.

PHOTOGRAPHY CREDITS

Bottle images: Ixcateco 89; Real Minero 90, 123; Augurio 94; Fane Katsini 96; Siete Misteros 98; Viejo Indecente 100; Pensador 101; Scorpion 103; Salvadores 104; Ilegal 106, 120; Los Danzantes 109; Derrumbes 111, 118; Ultramundo 113; Alipús 116; Cuentacuentos 117; Don Fulano 138, 147; Fortaleza 141; El Rayo 142; Tequila Ocho 144; Arette 145; Cascahuin 146; La Venenosa 156, 160; El Viaje 158; La Xamana 159; Santo Cuviso 169; Parejo 176; Desert Door 178.

Tyler Nilson 6; Cuentacuentos 21 (right). All other photography by Anna Bruce.